Max Huber

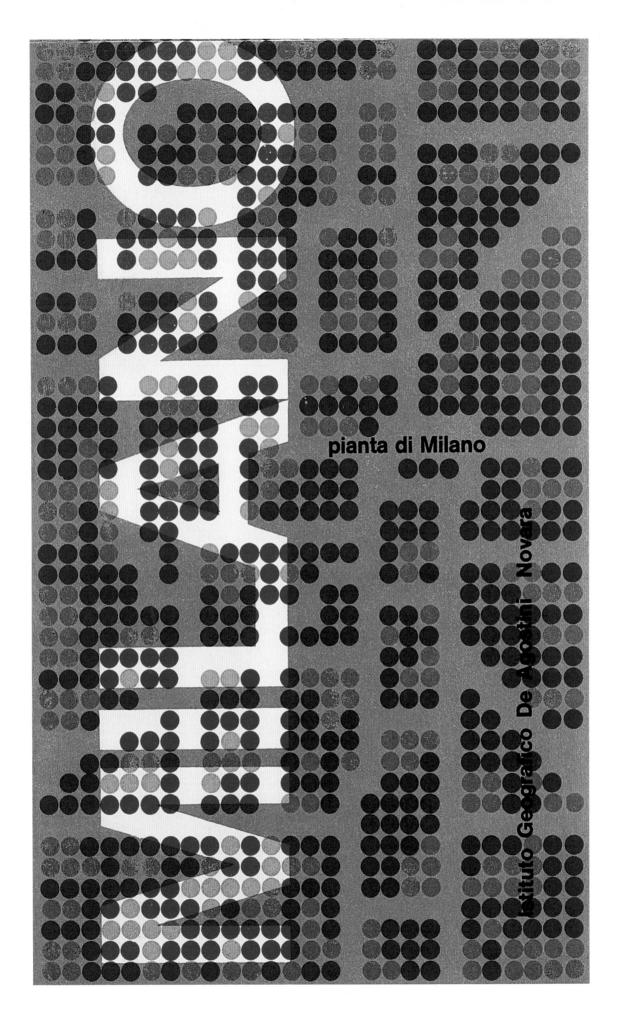

pianta di Milano

Istituto Geografico De Agostini Novara

Max Huber

Stanislaus von Moos
Mara Campana
Giampiero Bosoni

Phaidon Press Limited
Regent's Wharf
All Saints Street
London N1 9PA

Phaidon Press Inc.
180 Varick Street
New York, NY 10014

www.phaidon.com

First published 2006
© 2006 Phaidon Press
Limited

ISBN 0 7148 4547 7

A CIP Catalogue record for
this book is available from
the British Library

Essay One translated by
Steven Lindberg
Essays Two and Three,
and Portfolio introductions
translated by Barbara Fisher

Designed by
Hans Dieter Reichert
Printed in Hong Kong

Contents

Work Aesthetic and Mass Consumption:
The Art of Max Huber
Stanislaus von Moos

Max Huber
1940s

1

Work Aesthetic and Mass Consumption:
The Art of Max Huber

Stanislaus von Moos

The Birth of a Logo

Few incidents throw as much light on Huber's place in the complex post-war world of 'symbol, communication and consumption'[1] as does his first visit to Studio Boggeri in Milan of December 1940. He was just twenty-one years old and barely capable of stuttering a few words in Italian. The elegant calling card he left behind appears to be printed, but on closer examination it becomes clear that it has been meticulously executed by hand. When Antonio Boggeri spotted the illusion, he immediately hired the young visitor.[2] Most likely he was beguiled not only by the technical perfection of the lettering, but also by the careful spacing of the characters and the motif of tangled white lines on a black field that is so precisely arranged within the format of the card. Boggeri later adopted the motif as the logo for his firm, adding a drawing hand and the handwritten name 'Studio Boggeri'.

One cannot help but think of Max Bill's *Fünfzehn Variationen über ein Thema* (Fifteen Variations on a Theme, 1935–8) in this context, a work that Huber probably knew – just as Bill himself seems to have been familiar with Marcel Duchamp's *Rotary Demisphere* when he conceived his series. In one of Bill's variations the spiral looks like the trace of an irregularly swinging circular movement, but this seemingly irrational 'reeling' obeys a strict system, as Bill elucidated in his caption.[3] Huber achieved a similar effect but was apparently not attempting to make it appear to be the result of a geometrical calculation. Instead, the tangle looks like the result of a playful, experimental hand movement – an effect that was later reinforced on the Studio Boggeri business card by the addition of the drawing hand. In this way the discipline of graphic design is illustrated through its classic instruments while simultaneously seeming to reflect on itself through these looping forms.

opposite top
La Rinascente
logo on window shop
1950s

opposite bottom
COIN
sign, 1950s

top left
Marcel Duchamp
**Rotary Demisphere
(Precision Optics)**
motorized optical device,
1920
1486 x 642 x 609 mm

top right
Max Bill
**Variation Fifteen from
Fifteen Variations on a
Theme**
lithograph, 1935–8
305 x 320 mm

bottom
Handmade calling card
1951
60 x 135 mm

Such finicky and introverted experiments with geometry and three-dimensionality are the alpha and omega of the New Graphic Art – or indeed of Concrete Art in general – which would accompany Huber throughout his life. As to the emphatically extroverted rhetoric of his art, his delight in the colourful and the spectacular, it is difficult not to relate them to the Milanese context. When speaking, in his 'Futurist Manifesto' in 1909, of the 'multicoloured and polyphonic tides of revolutions in the modern capitals', Filippo Marinetti could not have foreseen the *teatri di massa* (theatre of masses) of Fascism, and much less the apparently de-politicized but no less belligerent spectacles of Italy's post-war economic boom.[4] And while it is true that, in the advertising work of Huber, Albe Steiner, Bruno Munari or Franco Grignani, the Futurist *genius loci* appears subverted, if not substituted, by the more serene and less politically compromised tradition of Milanese avant-garde art as represented by such artists as Mauro Reggiani, Fausto Melotti, Luigi Veronesi and Munari himself[5] (and, more specifically, by Huber's puritanical, constructivist Swiss background), the visual punctuations that brought Huber fame – the logos of La Rinascente, Esselunga or Coin, to mention but a few – unambiguously reverberate with Marinetti's rabble-rousing *parole in libertà* (words in freedom).

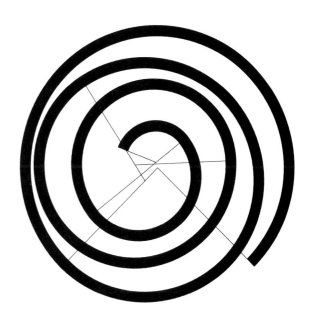

huber

max

foto

baar · inwilerstrasse

grafik

On a pedestal
advertisement for Gold
Stripe Nylon, featured in
The Mechanical Bride by
Marshall McLuhan, 1967

The Bauhaus Tradition versus the Hidden Persuaders

The presence of the Futurist legacy in Huber's work – despite the apparent
lack of a direct dialogue with this tradition – suggests that before exploring
Huber's art in terms of its own premises it may be useful to adopt a more
distant vantage point so as to grasp synthetically what his work *was* and what
it was *not.* Some key themes in advertising, for example, are so conspicuously
absent from Huber's imaginary that one is tempted to draw a phantom
portrait of them from the blank spots they leave behind. At least two of these
themes are distinctly connected to the European love-hate relationship with
American mass culture. The first (typically 'low') draws on the human drive for
pleasure, profit and sex – in short, the proverbial ingredients of the non-
Madison-Avenue-based American advertisement as practised by the legendary
'hidden persuaders'.[6] The second (distinctly 'high') is influenced by Surrealism
and tends to subordinate the content of the message to the point of gimmickry. Two authorities can illuminate these respective topics: the Canadian
media guru Marshall McLuhan and the German art historian Alexander Dorner.

In a lecture of 1987, Huber explicitly referred to McLuhan, citing his idea
that an infant, sitting on his high chair and watching television, gleans far
more information from all over the world than his grandparents would have
absorbed throughout their entire lives.[7] Considering Huber's lucid self-
assessment as an 'artisan' in the age of the already inexhaustible media
bustle, or – as he once put it – an 'artisanal worker, more or less belonging
to the prehistory of visual communication',[8] it should come as no surprise that
he was familiar with such themes. He may or may not have known about
McLuhan's comments on American advertising strategies, published some
time before the work on electronic communication that was to make the latter
famous. Commenting on an advertisement from which he took the title of one
of his early books, *The Mechanical Bride: Folklore of Industrial Man* of 1951,
McLuhan wrote: 'To the mind of the modern girl, legs, like busts, are power
points, which she has been taught to tailor, but as parts of the success kit
rather than erotically or sensuously.'[9] According to McLuhan, the modern girl
uses her legs – thanks to the ingenious invention of nylon stockings – as
'display objects', that is, as external ornaments comparable, for example, to
the grille of a car in an advertisement.

Quite independently of McLuhan, and indeed earlier than him (from 1947
onwards), the British painter and sculptor Eduardo Paolozzi made this
aggressive iconography of industrial standardization and sex the point of
departure for his artistic paraphrases – or more precisely, parodies – of
American mass culture. Somewhat later, Richard Hamilton pushed the theme
even further in paintings like *Hommage à Chrysler Corp.* (1957) and *Hers
Is a Lush Situation* (1958).[10] As if to close the circle, around 1960 the graphic
artist Herbert Bayer would make the stereotypical American 'consumer fet-
ishes' that had reared their ugly heads in the works of Paolozzi and Hamilton
(the pin-up girl, the flashy car and all the trappings of the American
dreamland) the object of an anti-consumerist protest collage.[11] Albeit with
different intent, such images epitomize what the ideologues of the New
Graphic Art found so offensive about American advertising, when they took
a stand, for example, against the sentimental 'storytelling' of American
magazine advertisements and against the cynicism of American 'Marketing'
and 'Motivation Research' (a polemic particularly cherished by Huber).[12]

As for the Surrealist-influenced strand in advertising, it is enough to recall
how Salvador Dalí triggered an explosive mixture of fascination and disgust
in the public during the post-war period by transgressing this line between
high art and mass culture. In *The Way Beyond 'Art'* (1947), Alexander Dorner
discusses this theme in relation to the work of Bayer, which makes his book
all the more interesting in our context.[13] Dorner wonders at the astonishing
success of Surrealism in the advertising of the period. Under the sign

of Surrealism the offer of merchandise had become a 'frivolous, almost undignified display of stagnant superfluity'. Why should we be caught up in this 'confusing hothouse atmosphere', he asks, rather than reject this 'chaotic autonomy of the world of the "free individual"'.[14] Dorner did not name names, but his polemic against 'retrogressive Surrealism' was, of course, directed at Salvador Dalí, alias 'Avida Dollars', as André Breton called his former ally. With his window displays on Fifth Avenue, the Venus Pavilion at the New York World Fair in 1939, stage sets for Hollywood productions such as Alfred Hitchcock's *Spellbound*, a cover for *Vogue* and so on, Dalí played a lively role in the commercialization of this art movement.[15]

What irritated (not to say disgusted) the Bauhaus-man Dorner most was the strangely asocial role Surrealism played, and the naivety with which the business world adopted its cynical and ironic tone. But ultimately the problem was – in his eyes – that the Surrealist imagery severed the domain of consumption from the world of the factory, the aesthetic of the commodity from the logic of industrial production. 'Why should the artist's self-expression step between public and producer?', he asked. Why should the viewer's attention be 'diverted' from the vital process of living (which is the basis for the whole system of industrial production)? 'Why shouldn't it rather inform that process with individual energies and show the production and consumption of goods as part of the higher functionalism of growing life in universally recognizable signs?'[16] The question is, of course, rhetorical, and in the book the answer is given through the work of Bayer. According to Dorner, Bayer is the man who manages to make this 'higher functionalism of growing life' visible 'in universally recognizable signs'.

A Logic of Economy and Ornament

If Dorner had been living in Italy, he might have chosen Huber rather than Bayer as his star witness. Huber's programme largely corresponded to that of his somewhat older colleague, who had emigrated to the United States in 1938. As was true of Bayer's work, Huber's appears like a bastion against the banality of an advertising culture that is content with naturalistic representations of consumption – either figurative or narrative – or with the extravagance of paradox and gimmickry for their own sake. Based upon the aesthetic strategies of Constructivism and of Concrete Art, Huber's art enthusiastically joins in the disciplined world of aesthetic modernity in that it subordinates even the most modest of messages to an elaborate logic of economy and of ornament.

The rhetoric of the pun, literary or visual i.e. the principle of economy applied to advertising has been fascinating to high culture ever since Lamartine. And in some ways Leopold Bloom's nocturnal 'cogitations', as described in James Joyce's *Ulysses*, reflect themes that obsessed Guillaume Apollinaire ('the commercial brochures, the catalogues, the posters that sing so loudly. Here is this morning's poetry') as much as they fascinated Robert and Sonia Delaunay or Fernand Léger – not to mention El Lissitzky. In Joyce's words:

the infinite possibilities hitherto unexploited of the modern art of advertisement if condensed in triliteral monoideal symbols, vertically of maximum visibility (divined), horizontally of maximum legibility (deciphered) and of magnetizing efficacy to arrest involuntary attention, to interest, to convince, to decide.
Such as?
K. 11. Kino's 11/- Trousers.
House of Keys. Alexander J. Keyes.

Returning to Huber, *IR* (La Rinascente), Esselunga and COIN – to mention but three of his emblematic inventions – are variations on the same theme.

In their own terms, these logos represent the cultured antidote to what Bloom in his cogitations cites as the graded epitome of banality:

> Such as not?
> Look at this long candle. Calculate when it burns out and you receive gratis one pair of our special no-compo-boots, guaranteed one candle power … (etc.)
> Such as never?
> What is home without Plumtree's Potted Meat?
> Incomplete … (etc.)

And Joyce again, on Leopold Bloom:

> What were habitually his final meditations?
> Of some one sole unique advertisement to cause passers to stop in wonder, a poster novelty, with all extraneous excretions excluded, reduced to its simplest and most efficient terms not exceeding the span of casual vision and congruous with the velocity of modern life.[17]

As for the question of ornament, it is fair to say that the entire project of modernism – including Loos' famously ambiguous diatribe against ornament as crime – implied a vision of modernity in which art, based on pure, abstract form and the elementary laws of perception, would ultimately merge with contemporary techniques and with lifestyle in order to form a visual continuum within which the whole era would recognize itself. As a rare cocktail of Constructivist and Abstract-Concrete delicacies, Huber's entire work appears to be committed to this utopia – apparently still unfettered by the psychological and cultural disruptions of the post-modern condition.[18]

Swiss Background

A closer look at Huber's work inevitably reveals the importance of his Swiss background. Having been educated in Zurich as a graphic artist and photographer, Huber found work with Studio Boggeri in Milan for a few months during the winter of 1940–1. Then, in 1945, when the war ended, he decided to emigrate permanently to Milan, where, thanks to his talent, his professionalism and his commitment, he became the 'crucial figure of Italian graphic art' in the 1950s.[19]

Zurich and Swiss graphic arts had become well known in Milan by 1936, when Max Bill designed the Swiss section of the 6th Milan Triennale. After 1945, when Italy's progressive cultural figures intensified their search for points of contact with a modernism uncompromised by the Fascist legacy, this aura around Zurich became even stronger. For the modern movement as a whole, Zurich was an important address, perhaps even one of the 'first sites of modernity', as Cornelius van Eesteren, the municipal architect of Amsterdam, wrote in 1936.[20] This status derived both from a solid tradition of industrial precision and from a tendency characteristic of Zurich to welcome unconventional guests within the city's walls – so long as they didn't disturb the natives. During the First World War, for example, Zurich became the base for many exiles, including Dadaists and James Joyce – not to mention Vladimir Lenin. A later 'guest' was El Lissitzky, who in 1925 edited the book *Kunst-Ismen*, and in 1929 curated the important 'Russische Ausstellung' (Russian Exhibition) at the Schweizerisches Landesmuseum, which was then the home of the Kunstgewerbeschule Zürich (Zurich School of Arts and Crafts). It was here that Hans Finsler established a photography department in 1932 – the very year the Bauhaus was forced to close down in Berlin – which helped the school to acquire a solid reputation as the heir of the Bauhaus tradition.[21] When Huber registered for the preliminary course in 1935 at the age of sixteen, the school had only just moved to its new premises, a large

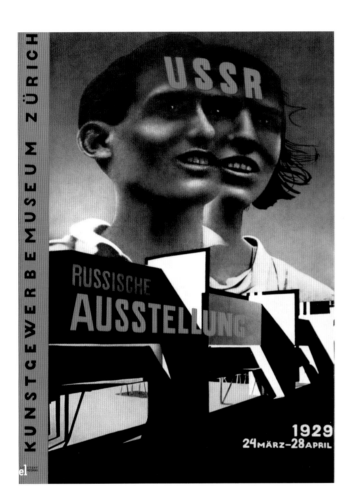

El Lissitzky
**Russische Ausstellung
(Russian Exhibition)**
poster,
Kunstgewerbemuseum,
Zurich, 1929
900 x 1280 mm

functionalist building in the New Objectivity style. The school's most important figure at this time was Alfred Willimann, a trained sculptor and type designer, who had just been hired by Finsler to teach photography. Internationally connected, thanks to his membership of the Parisian group Abstraction-Création, this fascinating teacher gave his students inspiration that would endure throughout their lives. Zurich's art and design world did not lack for stimuli at this time. Around 1932–3, it had already become a kind of interim station for a number of Bauhaus people who had been derailed by the National Socialist seizure of power in Germany. Sigfried Giedion, the art historian who coordinated CIAM (Congrès Internationaux d'Architecture Moderne – International Congress of Modern Architecture) from his Doldertal villa, brought the architect Marcel Breuer and graphic artist Herbert Bayer to Zurich and arranged commissions for them (both Breuer and Bayer later continued on to the United States, the former via England). Hans Girsberger, in turn, began the publication of Le Corbusier's complete works in the city, and in 1940 the architect Alfred Roth published a handbook called *Die neue Architektur* that would set the standard in the field of architectural publishing for years to come.[22] By then, graphic artists like Walter Cyliax, Jan Tschichold and Anton Stankowski, all from Germany, had already settled in Switzerland, and together with several younger Swiss colleagues – Max Bill and Richard Paul Lohse being the most important – laid the foundations for what was later referred to as the Swiss School of graphic design.[23] It was in the slipstream of this avant-garde scene that Huber began his career, working, for example, together with Emil Schulthess on the design of the monthly magazine *Du* at the Conzett & Huber publishing house (the name is purely coincidental), and preparing photo reportages in the style of his friend Werner Bischof. One of these documented the 'Schweizerische Landesausstellung' (Swiss National Fair) in Zurich in 1939 – an event that appears to have filled him with pride and enthusiasm.

As it turned out, a Zurich education proved to be a trump card, particularly in Milan – all the more so as that city, a centre of avant-garde art since Marinetti's day, lacked its own trade school for graphic artists and photographers during the 1930s and 1940s.[24]

Towards a Typology of Graphic Work

How can graphic works be categorized? Should one follow a hierarchy of formats (from the newspaper advertisement via the brochure and the poster up to the exhibition installation)? Or should one proceed in terms of subject matter (cars, pharmaceutical products, textiles, books, etc.), through a typology of formal components (type, documentary photography, formal or photographic experiment, etc.) and their various combinations?[25] Such a typology of works can be productive only if the underlying criteria are clear. Assuming that Huber's works convey messages that are of interest not merely to the archivist but also to the cultural historian working, say, in the tradition of Aby Warburg's *Bilderatlas*, the best way would be to proceed by means of a mix of subject matter and rhetorical *topoi*.[26] In the case of Huber, such a procedure inevitably leads to key words that relate his work to the aesthetic and educational agenda of the Bauhaus period, as taught at the Kunstgewerbeschule Zürich, and to Huber's deeply rooted image of himself as an 'artisanal worker'.

'Work' may be considered Huber's key theme. *Die Arbeit* (Work) was the title of a photo report, published in 1939 i.e. at the age of twenty. It contains images of people at work: a close-up of a factory worker next to a farmer ploughing, for example, followed by a woman in a workshop. It also shows the boyish Huber himself, at work on a layout. All this was combined with texts by Lenin and Joseph Stalin on the same subject. Throughout his career Huber would fall back on the stock images of social reportage and on the rhetoric of the eyewitness report. The photographic icons of the international workers' movement are obviously part of his repertoire, in accordance with the ideological direction of the publishing houses for which he preferred to work in Zurich and with which he would be connected in Italy. That he followed on the avant-garde tradition – in, for example, the jacket for Vladimir Mayakovsky's verse poem *Lenin*, inspired by El Lissitzky and Aleksandr Rodchenko – was obviously part of his cultural and political message.

But while it is true that work is the central theme in Huber's visual language, and that the socialist workers' movement was his natural homeland, one cannot help but notice that only a small number of images show men or women at work. An image such as El Lissitzky's poster for the 'Russian Exhibition' in Zurich in 1929, whose most striking aspect is the male and female workers becoming one, found no echo in his work. This heroicizing of the socialist worker as it was later canonized in Soviet state art appears to have thoroughly compromised this type of political rhetoric in Huber's eyes.

It is true, however, that this abstinence was only partly Huber's choice. To a large degree, it was inherent in the nature of his work as an advertiser in a consumer society, which has little use for the heroism of workers. For this reason, *lavoro* ('work' in Italian), survived as a theme for Huber primarily in the context of *dopolavoro* ('after work' i.e. leisure time) – particularly in the guise of sport and music. As if to compensate for the disappearance of work from the consumerist repertoire, Huber's characters appear wilfully to exaggerate the acrobatics of athletic performance – as skiers or tennis players in advertisements for Sporthaus Fritsch in Zurich, or as golfers in a La Rinascente advertisement.[27] And perhaps it is not merely coincidence that Huber likes to picture another major aspect of *dopolavoro* – music (which for Huber meant, above all, jazz) – as a theatre of physical exertion.

La vita di Lenin raccontata in versi dal
più grande poeta della Rivoluzione russa.

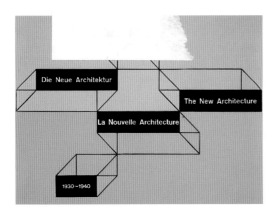

Constructivism and the Logic of Work

In his book on the architecture of revolutions Adolf Max Vogt has shown how work became an architectural theme after the Russian Revolution in 1917. It may seem obvious that this would occur in a political context obsessed with class struggle and with bringing about the victory of the working class. Vogt, however, goes beyond such generalities and defines work in terms of physics, as the 'exercise of energies along a given path'. Embodied as an 'enacted architectural process', the concept is crucial to projects by El Lissitzky, Vladimir Tatlin and the Vesnin brothers as 'provocatively acting architectural physics' – often rhetorically emphasized with the help of the 'counterdiagonal' (as in El Lissitzky's Lenin Tribune of 1919).[28]

Such Constructivist ideas run like a thread throughout Huber's oeuvre. Thus architecture, and above all, civil engineering, played a considerable role for him. Industry, epitomized by factory smokestacks and audacious iron-framework constructions, dynamically heightened through the effective use of a worm's-eye view that recalls Rodchenko or László Moholy-Nagy, is a key theme in his early advertising work. This was cxcmplified early on by a poster design for General Motors from 1938 that makes Biel, where General Motors assembled its cars for the Swiss market, look like Switzerland's answer to Detroit.[29]

What turns El Lissitzky's poster for the Zurich exhibition into a manifesto for collective optimism is not merely the pathos of the working-class couple but rather the lightweight construction of white panels in the lower part of the image. It symbolizes, in the language of the Neues Bauen movement, modernity in general, which was in turn synonymous with social progress. No wonder, then, that the mere scale of the planning and building projects underway in the Soviet Union at that time (as part of the first Five-Year Plan of 1928) attracted several Swiss architects to Russia. With the New York Stock

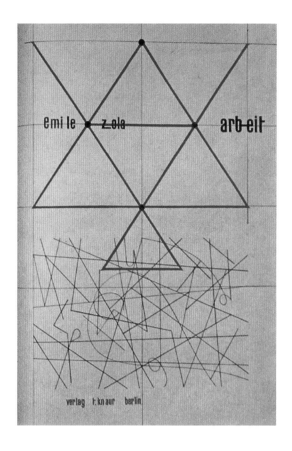

Exchange crash of 1929 it seemed obvious that the centre of modernism had shifted to the East, towards Moscow. Once there, however, these architects found their Constructivist dreams rapidly caught up in the reality of a comparatively undeveloped system of industrial production, and in a concept of cultural politics that clung to the celebration of regional identity and tradition.[30] Thus the internationalist ethos of Neues Bauen turned out to have a more realistic chance for development in the capitalist West than in the East – at least in the medium term. In this context, Zurich, the headquarters of CIAM, appeared as an interesting architectural laboratory, even if the relevant experiments – oscillating between the fine Werkbund housing colony in Zürich-Neubühl[31] and the more elegant Doldertal flats built somewhat later – were limited to the culturally enlightened middle class and bourgeoisie.[32]

In the canonical photographs of such projects, as well as in the advertising brochures of Wohnbedarf – a firm founded by Giedion, Werner Moser, Rudolf Steiger and other affiliated promoters of the new lifestyle[33] – the new architecture and its accoutrements appear to depict nothing so much as the logic of their own construction. The man who found the most emblematic graphic formulas for this way of reading Neues Bauen was undoubtedly Max Bill. While his humorous advertisements for Bau-Kredit Zürich AG, a middle-class bank that helped working people to build their own homes, illustrate the theme by way of naturalist sketches, the book jacket of Alfred Roth's *The New Architecture* translates it into an abstract, or indeed concrete, composition. This is where Huber's design for a German edition of Emile Zola's *Travail* (Work) appears to take off – were it not for the fact that it has an even more obvious source in Bill's sculpture *Konstruktion im Raum* (Construction in Space, 1938–9).[34] Or should one point straight to Paul Klee, Bill's most important teacher at the Bauhaus?

opposite top
Max Bill
The New Architecture
book cover, Dr H Gisberger, 1940
235 x 290 mm

opposite centre
Herbert Bayer
Wohnbedarf
catalogue cover, c. 1932
130 x 180 mm

opposite bottom
Max Bill
Konstruktion aus 30 Gleichen Elementen (Structure Made of 30 Identical Elements)
sculpture, c. 1937
459 x 76 x 153 cm

top
Arbeit (Work)
study for book cover, Knaur, 1939
dimensions unknown

bottom
La ricostruzione edilizia nell'U.R.S.S. (Building Reconstruction in the USSR)
book cover, Einaudi, 1946
210 x 300 mm

il petrolio
oggi

Nicolò Pignatelli Aragona

GULF ITALIA COMPANY

opposite
**Il petrolio oggi
(Today's Oil)**
brochure cover, 1960
215 x 190 mm

right
General Motors Suisse
study for advertisement,
1937
305 x 185 mm

left
László Moholy-Nagy
**View from the Berlin
Radio Tower**
photograph, 1928
dimensions unknown

Hands and the World of the Artisan

Roland Barthes has noted that the plates contained in the *Encyclopédie* of Denis Diderot and Jean le Rond d'Alembert (1751–76), frequently depict hands – sharpening nails, cutting corks, etc. – as if to emphasize the fact that the very activities which were being industrialized in the eighteenth century were rooted in the handicrafts. As Barthes has put it: 'hands, severed from the body, flutter around the work … these hands are doubtless the symbol of an artisanal world.'[35] Constructivism reactivated the theme – in the form, for example, of the hand holding a compass in El Lissitzky's logo for the architecture department of the Vkhutemas school (1928).[36] Given Huber's interest in work, as well as in naturalistic representation, it comes as no surprise that his advertisements would be linked – either directly or via El Lissitzky and Moholy-Nagy – to the tradition of the *Encyclopédie* by drawing attention to the hand holding the tool (like the stylized hand of a draftsman holding a pencil on Studio Boggeri's business card). It is in such a way that the commodities and services they advertised were anchored in the context of the activities they performed – whether in the workshop or laboratory or at home.

In images of industrialized production processes, however, it is only natural that the hand is conspicuously hidden away, as in countless advertisements, brochures and catalogues for the textile industry. No industry is as viscerally associated with the logic of fashion and the display of luxury as this one, and it is therefore all the more striking that Huber's advertising materials should undercut this logic by presenting not the product but the process of its manufacture (the spinning of yarn, the stacking of rolls of fabric, etc.). These campaigns are conceived not as an enticement to luxury and consumption, but rather, in the vein of the *Encyclopédie*, almost as a pedagogical project. The sphere that interests, once again, is the factory and the warehouse, not the shop window or the party; the world of production, not the spectacle of consumption.

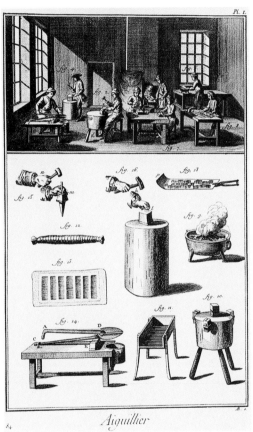

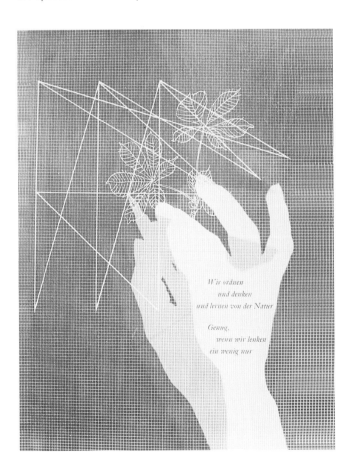

top
Max Huber for Studio
Boggeri
Ostelin Glaxo
study for advertisement,
1941
205 x 295 mm

bottom left
Rassegna Grafica
magazine cover, 1956
300 x 210 mm

bottom right
Stoffels
advertisement, c. 1940
125 x 170 mm

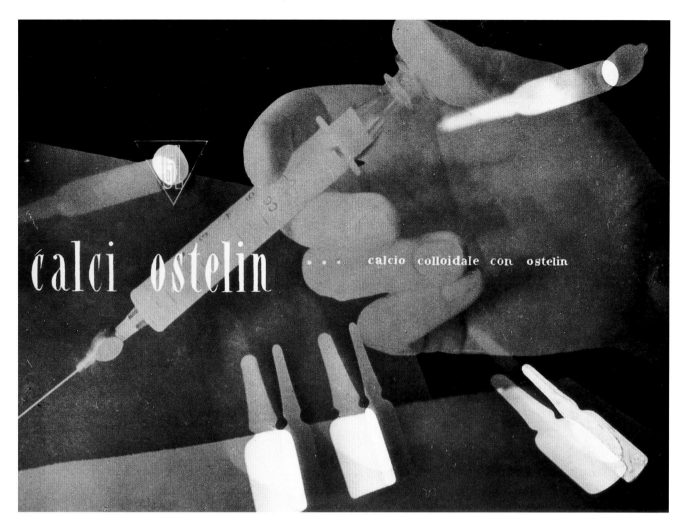

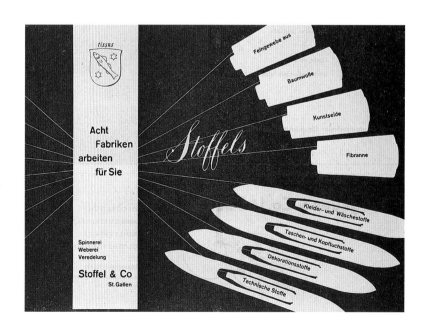

top
Tourist Publicity Campaign
study for poster, 1939
295 x 210 mm

bottom
Hans Erni
Die Schweiz, Ferienland der Völker (Switzerland: Playground of the People)
mural, Schweizerische Landesausstellung, Zurich, 1939 (detail)
6.5 x 108 m

Between Pictorialism, Folk Art and Techno-Culture

Huber's numerous tributes to the beauty of nature – scenic mountain tours, flowers, butterflies, etc. – beginning around 1939 are a natural counterpoint to his Constructivist fixation on production: they evoke leisure-time paradises for the working and middle classes. It is no coincidence that on the eve of the Second World War, a more relaxed, widely acceptable set of imagery as well as relatively more conventional forms of graphic layout were becoming increasingly important – as Huber's elegant design for the cover of *Das Werk* (Work) from 1939 illustrates. The main motif is a photograph of a living room showing functional furniture and wide windows with the typically wooden frames of the *Landistil*. A diagonally cropped, light blue plane frames this image like a *passe-partout*, providing a backdrop for the skilfully arranged typography. Huber here returns to the 'classical' use of photography and typography – including the underlying cropped plane of colour – proposing a solution that, through its tamed modernity, marks a distance from the formal radicality of the avant-garde.

The term *Landistil* represents an entire epoch in Swiss art history. The word comes from the *Landi*, the nickname of the Schweizerische Landesausstellung (Swiss National Fair) of 1939. Given the historical moment – 1939 – the exhibition would later take on almost mythical proportions in the nation's self-assessment. Its success was partly due to its insistence on a style in architecture, public art and mass culture that aimed to be distinctly Swiss by avoiding the Neoclassical pomposity of state art adopted in its neighbouring countries.[37] Hans Hofmann, the chief architect of the exhibition, gave it an overall look that could be described as a cultivated synthesis of Neues Bauen with elements of a Scandinavian-inspired regionalism – a style that belongs to the larger context of what Nikolaus Pevsner called the New Empiricism.[38] The visual arts primarily took on the form of historicizing murals and monumental figurative sculpture; Bill and his avant-garde friends had to be satisfied with graphic jobs. In fact, the precarious status of Switzerland,

surrounded on three sides by the axis powers, had fostered an astonishing degree of cultural consensus between the rural-based conservative middle class and the more urbanized segments of society, and also between Right and Left, and the *Landi* seemed like an adequate reflection of that consensus. The paradox is that the idealism of this project was partly subverted by a not so idealistic *Realpolitik*, in that we now know that the country's relative economic prosperity and cultural autonomy were conditioned by a considerable readiness to compromise politically with Germany.

One work stood out from the somewhat conventional sphere of Swiss art at the *Landi* – and not just because of its unusual dimensions (6.5 × 108 m): Hans Erni's monumental mural *Die Schweiz, Ferienland der Völker* (Switzerland: Playground of the People). A variation on the genre of the tourist brochure, the colossal mural was nothing less than the artist's attempt to present a bold cultural history of industrial Switzerland. The upper edge depicts the Alps as a frieze, in the crystal-clear weather of *foehn* wind conditions. Below that are views of the Swiss midlands and Ticino with its lakes. The peaks of the Bernese Alps are seen from the perspective of shaded valleys. A glider floats silently above the lower Alps of Ticino; it takes our gaze into the heights and from there Lake Lugano is seen as on a map. The foreground and middle ground of this immense painting are taken up with a quasi-cinematographic montage of views into the depth and others that draw the vantage point close to the viewer again. From the depths of the earth the mountain water flows out towards us through a trough carved from a trunk, depicted through extreme foreshortening. A little further to the right it collects in the pipeline that taps the reservoir to feed the turbine of the power station that provides the power for the Red Arrow, an electric motorcar from the Swiss railway that is gliding past. Elsewhere, an immense alphorn floats through the sky. A little further left Lötschental masks – emblematic icons of Swiss Folk art – grin beyond the horizon, while two butterflies glitter above the road over the Susten Pass, and a Swissair Douglas DC3 comes into view from out of a thicket of ferns and leaves.

top
Herbert Bayer
Can Our Cities Survive?
book cover, CIAM and
Harvard University Press,
1941
235 x 310 mm

bottom
László Moholy-Nagy
Pneumatik
study for poster, c. 1926
dimensions unknown

The theme of this work is the Swiss landscape in the changing seasons, combined with images from art history, the lives of the people and signs of the current techno-culture. Perhaps the abrupt contrast between small and large, old and new, is intended to make the viewer aware of the social contradictions of modern Switzerland. Konrad Farner, a Marxist cultural historian who had actively participated in formulating a programme for the painting, later observed that 'the railway leads to other destinations than the old road; the turbines cannot be brought in harmony with the procession, unless human consciousness splits or human thought stops before drawing the ultimate conclusions.'[39] It is tempting, however, to cling to a more literal understanding of the painting as an immense tableau using the means of modern art to portray Switzerland as a prototypical holiday landscape. Seen in this way, the railway depicted does not 'lead to other destinations than the old road' – rather, it serves to bring the crowds of hikers from the city to the country road, where they can view the spectacles of religious folklore and historical architecture.

Huber was one of the young artists who assisted Erni in painting the mural.[40] This close contact with the brilliant illustrator, who was also a declared artistic voice of the Left, must have had a lasting influence on the nineteen year old. More than any of his other teachers, Erni could have shown him how his art could benefit from the study of nature.[41] The studies for tourist posters that Huber produced around 1939 are inconceivable without Erni's model, and so is a design for a political poster – *Der Weg nach links* (The Way towards the Left) – which employs the very montage principle that some critics thought they found in the *Landi* painting.

Max Bill and Allegory

In contrast to his contemporary and antipode Erni, Bill was not a master of naturalistic illustration but a pioneer of Constructive and Concrete Art and art theory. It is thus only logical that his major works, like the sculpture *Kontinuität* (Continuity) (1947) for example, should be seen primarily as embodiments of his programme for Concrete Art, as well as part of a broad stream of non-objective sculpture in the twentieth century.[42] However, at least in one respect the two artists seem comparable – namely in their pronounced penchant for idealistic allegory.

Seen in this light, the Möbius strip of Bill's *Kontinuität* appears to be something more than just a sculptural variation on an age-old formula for infinity. Rather, one is tempted to view it as an artistic metaphor for one of the universal myths of the post-war period: the *panta rhei* of limitless mobility. Infinite loops of modern roads and highways over mountain passes run through several book jackets and posters by Bayer and Herbert Matter from the 1930s onwards. Admittedly, Huber's advertisement for a linoleum manufacturer of c. 1940 thematized the infinite loop of a moulded material used for flooring in offices and homes, alluding only indirectly to the experience of street traffic – in contrast to an advertisement for the road construction company Puricelli of c. 1948.

His famous poster for the Gran Premio di Monza (Monza Grand Prix) (1948) is a classic on this theme. Although Moholy-Nagy's 1926 advertisement for Pneumatik tyres anticipated important aspects of this visual trope, by comparison it is little more than a first attempt to walk on uncertain ground. Huber both clarified the idea and made it more Italian. By adding a red-and-blue arrow, he gave a direction to the curve of the street, defining it in the best tradition of Marinetti ('A racing car … is more beautiful than the Victory of Samothrace') as the battleground for a specifically Italian combination of machine and machismo. The type (reading 'Gran premio dell'Autodromo') that storms forth perspectively from the background underlines this effect. With this poster, Huber entered the pantheon of a specifically Italian mass art that

**Gran premio dell'
Autodromo Monza 1948
(Monza Grand Prix 1948)**
poster, 1948
1400 x 1000 mm

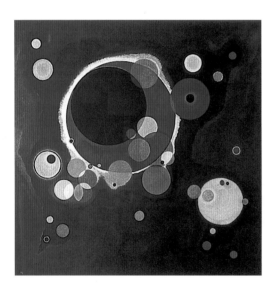

illustrates Ettore Sottsass's dictum of 1947: 'One can state calmly that the people of Greece would never have existed without the sea, and that the sea is their great story. I believe our great story, by contrast, is *velocità* (speed).'[43]

Concrete Art and the Logic of Work

While it is true that the sensuous kinaesthetics[44] of Huber's allegories of modernity relate to Bill as well as to Erni, his work is primarily connected to Concrete Art in a more conceptual way. For the theory of Concrete Art suggests that art can be seen as visually embodied work precisely when it is not evoking a representational idea.[45]

When in 1939 the decision was made to use the profits of the Swiss National Fair staged earlier that year to create a monument 'in honour of work' in Zurich's working-class district a competition was announced. To suggest that work can be embodied in a public monument without illustrating people at work may sound strange, but Karl Geiser's beautiful design ended up on top of the pile. It shows a working-class family strolling in the city with their shopping bags.[46] One can easily imagine the artist's (as well as the jury's) dilemma. A worker operating at his workbench or even worse a worker hero storming his way into the future would have been inconceivable in Zurich; that type of solution would have appeared synonymous with socialist, or more specifically Soviet, state art. Thus Geiser's solution seemed like a viable compromise.

Bill had also entered the competition, but with a project that exemplifies what a non-figurative representation of work might look like. It proposed a large, three-dimensional Swiss cross (4.2 x 1.3 x 1.6 m), inscribed in a cube with sides 4.2 m in length and composed of six elements of equal size. Eight identical cubes of the same material were to be placed next to it, corresponding to the masses of the volume that would remain if the cross were extracted from the cube. Smaller cubes of 40 cm were cut out of the larger cube and placed separately as blocks on which viewers could sit. As Bruno Reichlin has noted, the aesthetic event intended here consists in 'a generating, structuring, self-regulating principle that makes it clear through series, variations, transformations and rhythms that it is systematically exploring a form.'[47]

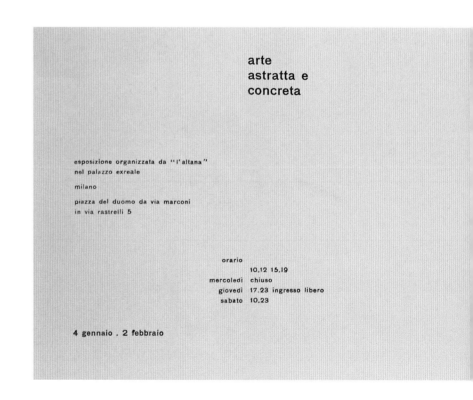

Bill appears to have viewed his proposal as a symbolic realization of one of the core ideas of the Landesausstellung of 1939, namely, that 'the high quality of Swiss work … represented a profession of faith in the fatherland', as the director of the *Landi*, Armin Meili, had put it.[48] The strict geometry and the standardization of the parts embodied the idea of industrial production. Hand imprints, notched into the cube in actual size, were intended to depict the indispensable contribution of skilled work to industry.

The allegory points to a more fundamental trope, for ultimately the principle of work can be said to be inherent from the start in Concrete Art. Such works embody the thought processes that brought them about. Ever since Kasimir Malevich created his *Black Square* in 1913 and – a little later – his *Black Circle*, reality in art has been conceived of in terms of the radically reduced forms of square and circle. Later, in 1922, Malevich's student El Lissitzky transformed the Suprematist *Urtext* of square and disk into a typographic game varying Mayakovsky's poem *Dlia golosa* (For the Voice). Thus entering a space in which the elementary geometrical sign appears as an ambiguous figure, capable of representing both the optical law that underlies its shape and traditional representational ideas.[49] The absoluteness of a large red dot thus becomes an emblem of the rising sun. A little pile of black squares next to the dot becomes the symbol of world civilization.

Bill did not go all the way back to Malevich when, in an article of 1944, he developed his theory by which the forms of Concrete Art are not abstracted from a representational idea but rather exist concretely as embodiments of ideas. His key example is Wassily Kandinsky's painting *Einige Kreise* (Several Circles) of 1926. Comparing the work to the 1940 painting by Klee *Schlamm-Assel-Fisch* (Mud-Woodlouse-Fish), Bill says:

> the essential difference is that the content and form of the image establish an autonomous artistic unity. Except that colour and composition generate tensions and inner moods, and except that the order does come to rest in itself and pulsate there, nothing else is relevant but what is present, what is visible. That the latter is synonymous with its content, and that it is based on an artistic volition cannot be discussed here in detail.[50]

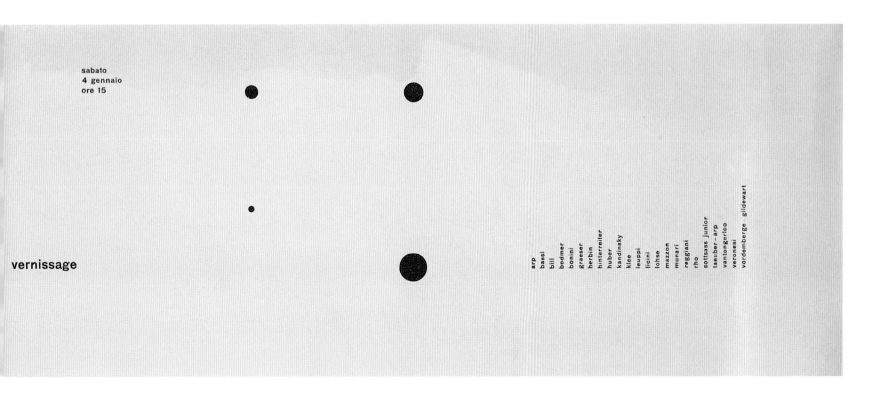

top
**Skizze für Kreisbild
(Sketches for a Circle
Painting)**
1942
410 x 410 mm

bottom left
Antonio Boggeri and Max
Huber
Studio Boggeri
exhibition panel based on
business card, 1940
1000 x 1000 mm

bottom right
**Procedimento CIM
per l'oscuramento
contro incursioni aeree
(CIM blackout for
bombing raids)**
leaflet, 1942
110 x 210 mm

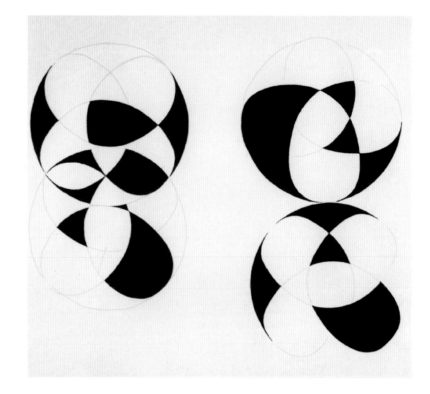

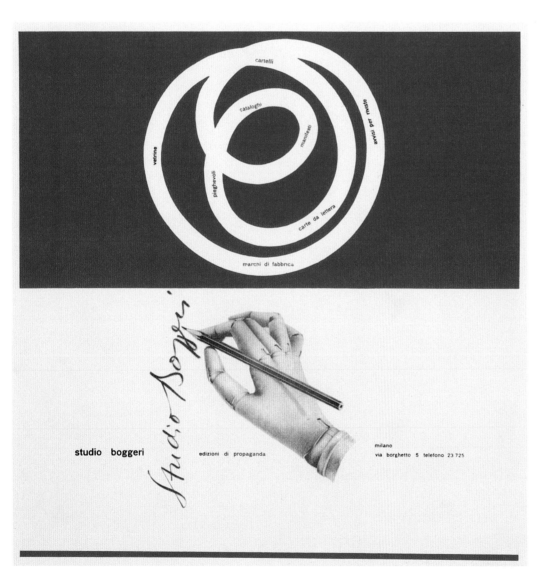

Interestingly, in the first version of the article, Bill had added a famous passage from Plato's dialogue with Philebos in order to clarify his point.[51]

He had presented his theory of *Konkrete Gestaltung* (Concrete Design) for the first time in 1936, in the catalogue for the exhibition 'Zeitprobleme der Schweizer Malerei und Plastik' (Contemporary Problems in Swiss Painting and Sculpture).[52] The phrase itself, however, was coined by Theo van Doesburg, and probably first used – in the sense that was later to become canonized – by Max Burchartz in 1924[53]. As a member of the artists' group Allianz,[54] Huber must have been familiar with such ideas at an early date – we know from his calling card of 1940 how much he was acquainted with the artistic methods developed in that context. When the members of the

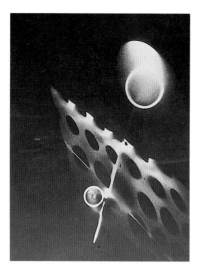

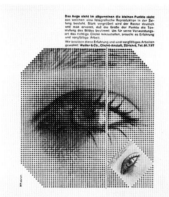

Milan artists' group Altana, together with Lanfranco Bombelli Tiravanti, decided to produce the exhibition 'Arte astratta e concreta' in Milan, it thus seemed only natural to entrust Huber with the design of the catalogue and the invitation card. Nor is it a surprise that Switzerland, and especially the circle around Bill, was assigned a central place in it.[55]

Concrete also means that the work's meaning is identical to the elements that constitute it. Concrete Art, in other words, narrates the laws by which it is generated. This may be why Huber, choosing Kandinsky's point and line to plane as his point of departure, showed nothing but a progression of four dots of various sizes distributed within the square for the 'Arte astratta e concreta' invitation. In his own work as a painter, however – perhaps inspired by Leo Leuppi or Hans Hinterreiter – he moved on to playing with more complex figurations.[56] An example is *Skizze für Kreisbild* (Sketches for a Circle Painting) of 1942, where he seems once again to play with the theme of Bill's *Fünfzehn Variationen*, but now in such a way that the circular movement of the planar segments produces the illusion of three-dimensional volume – much as in Duchamp's *Rotoreliefs*. Bill might have spoken of a 'concretion with a spatial character'.[57]

As if in reaction to this tendency towards ornamental complexity, in Huber's advertising work the Suprematist *Urtext* is reduced all the more intently to its elemental signal function. Here, dots and circles unfold their atavistic potential as elementary marks, as signs that often embody nothing but the appeal of pure form as spectacle in space (like rings and balls in the circus) – as in his glorious posters for Borsalino hats.

The Magic of Print and the Aesthetics of Reproduction
In pre-industrial times, the techniques by which works of art were reproduced and multiplied for a mass audience never really produced aesthetically neutral images. A woodcut, an etching or a lithograph cannot imitate its original to the point of deception. Such illusionism – the transparency of the medium with respect to the message – started to become possible only with photography, the oleograph and later the rotogravure, then with the four-colour print and

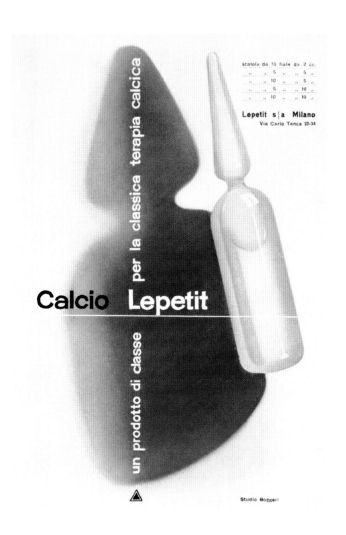

the Ciba print – to say nothing of today's extravagant possibilities of electronic simulation and animation.

By the 1920s, however, the emerging aesthetic neutrality of reproductions began to be subverted by an increasing fascination with the visual side-products of those new techniques – at least in the sphere of avant-garde art. Artists like Man Ray or Moholy-Nagy opened the eyes of their time to the visual mysteries that occur when everyday objects are reflected in the negative on a photographic plate or on film.[58] El Lissitzky was amongst those who applied such fascinations to the language of advertising at an early date. At the Kunstgewerbeschule Zürich these techniques were part of the curriculum. Huber would practice them throughout his entire lifetime. His first important exhibition design – the installation of the 8th Milan Triennale, in 1947 – is nothing so much as a variation on the theme of the photogram on the scale of scenography. Later, Huber's fascination with the materiality of film as a support for images took him so far as to produce a film poster with nothing but a colourful confetti of punched stripes of film – in provocative opposition to the inherently dramatic and theatrical trend of the genre. In 1964 he even advertised a 'Fashion Weekend' by merely arranging stripes of colour film on a light table. Nor should we be surprised that the principle of the dot screen – an invention without which modern image production would not exist

– turned out to be the springboard for some of Huber's most fascinating visual inventions.

Once again the path leads back to Bill. The Swiss section at the 6th Milan Triennale of 1936, with its monumental visual metaphor for screen printing (in the form of a massive wall of dots) and of paper production (in the form of a plaster loop hanging down from the ceiling) – gave the starting signal for Huber's own splendid variations on the theme of the image that illustrates nothing so much as the work that produced it. The logic of reproduction as reflected in the dot screen can be said to have become the 'automatic pilot' of the New Graphic Art. (Somewhat later, with artists like Gerhard Richter, Sigmar Polke, or Markus Raetz, the dot screen would even become a new form of automatic writing in art – but that is another story.)

The Cold War and the Call for Aesthetic Discipline

Such visual obsessions appear to imply a pedagogic agenda. For Huber, advertising – besides its primary role of marketing goods and services – seems in its aesthetic self-referentiality to be about awakening in consumers an awareness of ordinary things as human work translated into form. The very graphic media that bring those messages before the public illustrate the logic of mechanical and perceptual processes at work in everyday life. In this way, as Giovanni Anceschi has put it, this art even aims at directing 'our purchasing behaviour towards the most indispensable and most elementary goods – food, clothing – occasionally even including the urge to restrain consumer behaviour'.[59]

What, then, is Huber's place in the history of New Graphic Art? As far back as 1959, Karl Gerstner and Markus Kutter discussed the phase in the evolution of advertising styles to which Huber belongs, a history that was then already four decades long. 'The intended objectives are now met' so they summarize – not without a certain scepticism. 'Graphic art has fulfilled its programme'. And they continue: 'Advertising graphics has been cultivated, its level has been elevated.' But they also mention the cost involved: the fatal tendency towards 'levelling from above, the abandoning of intellectual work, of real grappling with the unsolved problem. With its adversaries gone, graphic art becomes … self-satisfied, merely refined, fastidious.'[60] The remark was not directed at Huber, of course, but at the general situation of the New Graphic Art and its crisis following modernism's universal breakthrough in the 1950s. Yet the risks of the situation appear to be embodied almost emblematically in Huber's work – indebted as it is, on the one hand, to a puritan tradition (Swiss) and following, on the other, a logic of playfulness and extroverted improvisation (Italian). With him, the aesthetic recipes of the avant garde, enriched by certain canonical icons of the workers' movement, appear to have blended seamlessly with the taste of an enlightened and liberal mainstream.

Is it wrong to suspect that this art, at least in its commitment to professional and aesthetic discipline, and in its determination to include the heritage of the artistic Left, reflects something of the rumblings of the Cold War? At least there is a political undertone in the defence put forward by Gerstner and Kutter of the Constructivist tradition of The New Graphic Art – a tradition to which GGK (Gerstner, Gredinger and Kutter), their own famous agency in Basle, was no less committed than Huber.

Though they appear to see some danger in this trend, they argue that the value attached to publicity is such that much thought must be devoted to the way it is used especially so in a world 'where free competition is the dynamic of the economic system and the distinguishing mark of cultural and political life' – as if the seriousness of the political situation would also imply a call towards the systematic and the transparency of means in advertising art. With the political and ideological constraints of the Cold War gone the legacy of Max Huber appears to have definitely entered the universe of art history.

Portfolio: Architecture and Design

Co-ordinated images for the advertisement and presentation of cultural events did not develop in Italy until after the Second World War. The poster, until then basically the only communication tool, was complemented by catalogues, advertisements and other materials, both in the Milan Triennale exhibitions and in Remo Muratore's extraordinary co-ordinated image for the Piccolo Teatro, which he began in 1959. With the 8th Milan Triennale of 1947, Max Huber became one of the pioneers of the design of co-ordinated images. This assignment later earned him a number of related commissions. Edizioni di Comunità (founded by Adriano Olivetti), Hoepli, Görlich Editore and the Ordine degli Architetti, as well as museums and art galleries, soon realised that the documentation of temporary events required the production of publications, such as catalogues and annals. This led to the new phenomenon of the specialist publisher. The monographic books that Huber produced on the work of some of the leading Italian architects remain unsurpassed lessons in design (copied in the 1980s by several Italian studios). The use of architects' design materials, layouts and elevations, combined with photographs of the built works over backgrounds of transparent colour (never more than two in addition to black), created a perfectly assembled page. Only if the subject was a photographer – Edward Steichen, Robert Capa, Werner Bischof, Paolo Monti – were photographs employed, although never manipulated out of respect for their work. The colour and compositional variations in the posters and books on Huber's own work are interesting, as for example in the group exhibition with the graphic artists Warja Lavater and Otto Teucher. In this case, it was not a photograph of their work that was used to identify them. The poster only displayed the names, graphically treated with coordinated colour and typography, as if the particular aesthetics of the graphic design could serve to represent them.

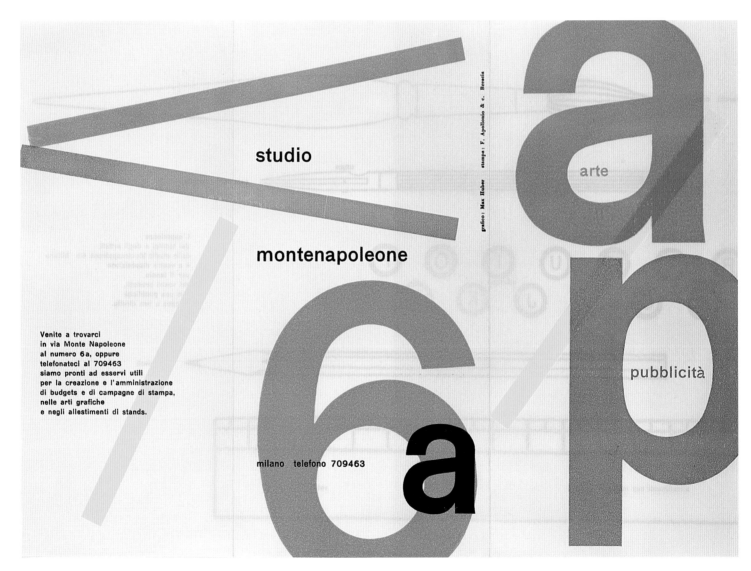

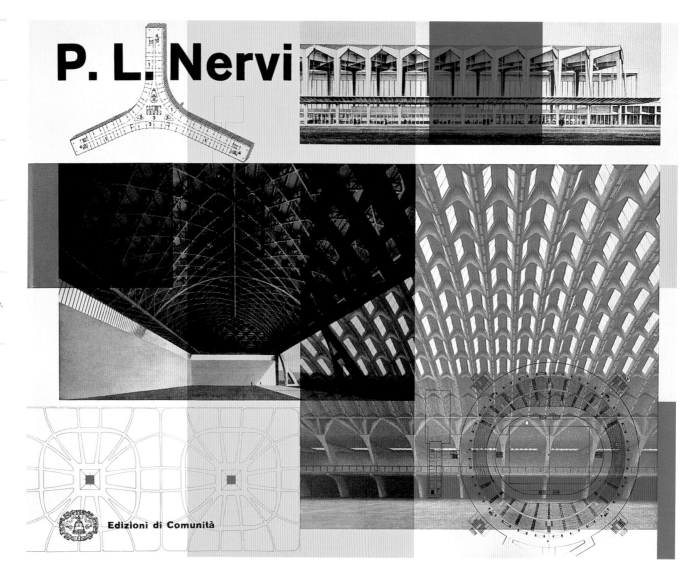

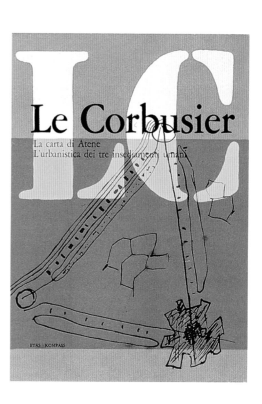

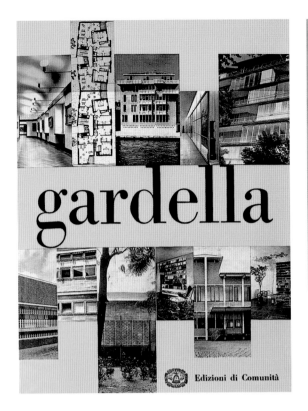

top left
Gardella
book cover, Edizoni di
Comunità, 1958
255 x 195 mm

top right
**La Famiglia dell'Uomo
(The Family of Man)**
poster, Civica Galleria
d'Arte Moderna, Milan, 1959
1000 x 700 mm

bottom left
Stile Industria
magazine cover, 1958
325 x 245 mm

bottom right
Stile Industria
magazine cover, 1960
325 x 245 mm

top left
Atti del collegio regionale lombardo degli architetti (Journal of the Lombard Association of Architects)
magazine cover, 1958
240 x 170 mm

top right
Christmas Card for Studio Castiglioni
1959
215 x 215 mm

bottom
Convegno su gli sviluppi di Milano (Convention on the Development of Milan)
poster, 1959
700 x 1000 mm

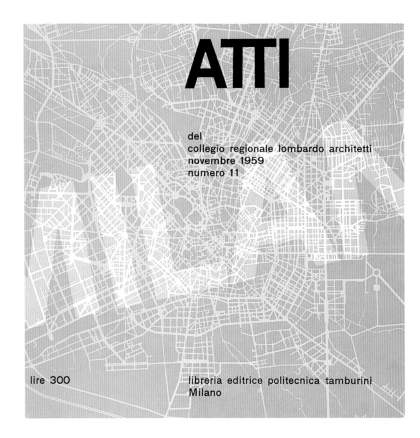

ATTI

del
collegio regionale lombardo architetti
novembre 1959
numero 11

lire 300

libreria editrice politecnica tamburini
Milano

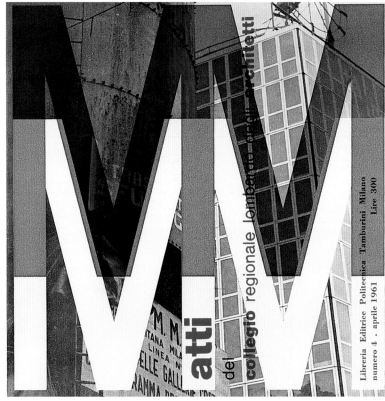

atti

del
collegio regionale lombardo degli architetti

Libreria Editrice Politecnica Tamburini Milano
Lire 300

numero 4 · aprile 1961

atti

del

collegio regionale lombardo degli architetti

Libreria
Editrice
Politecnica Tamburini
Milano

numero 9   settembre 1961
lire 300

atti

del collegio regionale lombardo degli architetti

Edizioni Ariminum
Milano

numero 1   gennaio 1962
lire 300

bottom and opposite
**Atti del collegio regionale
lombardo degli architetti
(Journal of the Lombard
Association of Architects)**
magazine covers, 1959-63
210 x 210 mm

atti
del collegio regionale lombardo degli architetti

Libreria Editrice
Politecnica Tamburini
Milano
numero 12 dicembre 1961
lire 300

Robert
Ente Manifestazioni Milanesi
CAPA
fotografie di guerra

Milano
palazzo Reale. giugno-luglio 1961

a. nava milano

Robert Capa: fotografie di
guerra (Robert Capa: War
Photography)
Palazzo Reale, Milan,
poster, 1961
500 x 350 mm

top
Calligraphy 1535–1885
book cover, La Bibliofila,
1962
245 x 370 mm

bottom left
**Sammlung des
Kunstgewerbemuseums
(Collection of the
Museum of Arts and
Crafts)**
poster, Museum Bellerive,
Zurich, 1969
1280 x 905 mm

bottom right
Glas (Glass)
poster, Museum Bellerive,
Zurich, 1969
1280 x 905 mm

galleria mosaico chiasso palazzo moretto

第13回＝デザイン・ギャラリー展

〈マックス・フーバーの

グラフィック・デザイン〉

exhibition 13 ....

'Max Huber and his graphic works'

マックス・フーバーはミラノで活躍している
イタリアの第一線デザイナー。東京で個展を
ひらき、皆さんに見ていただくのが、日本び
いきの彼の、数年来の希望でした。しかし、
それだけではありません。同氏はかつてミラ
ノのラ・リナシェンチ百貨店のアート・ディ
レクターとして、今日の基本線をうち出した
人物。その後、同百貨店が、コンパッソ・ド
ーロ賞などを創設、イタリアのデザイン運動
の一大拠点となっていることは、国際的にも
よく知られています。そういう意味でも、同
氏の個展が、日本のラ・リナシェンヂともい
うべき、銀座松屋を会場として開かれること
に、大きな意義が見いだせると思います。

勝見 勝

銀座店7階❽デザインギャラリー

主催＝日本デザインコミッティ

3月22日(月)ー4月14日(水)

銀座松屋

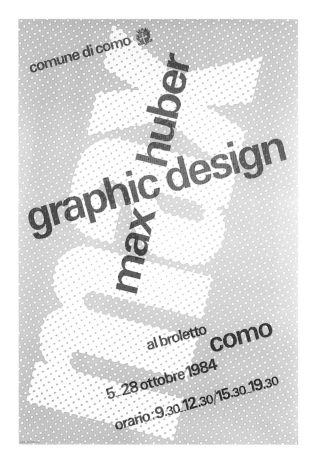

comune di como

graphic design

max huber

al broletto   como

5_28 ottobre 1984

orario : 9.30_12.30/15.30_19.30

opposite top
Max Huber Exhibition
poster, Galleria Mosaico,
Chiasso, 1971
265 x 480 mm

opposite bottom left
**Max Huber and His
Graphic Works**
invitation card, 1965
105 x 145 mm

opposite bottom right
**Max Huber Graphic
Design**
poster, Broletto, Como, 1984
700 x 1000 mm

right
**Max Huber: Progetti
grafici 1936–1981 (Max
Huber: Graphic Design
1936–81)**
book cover and slipcase,
Electa, 1982
240 x 220 mm

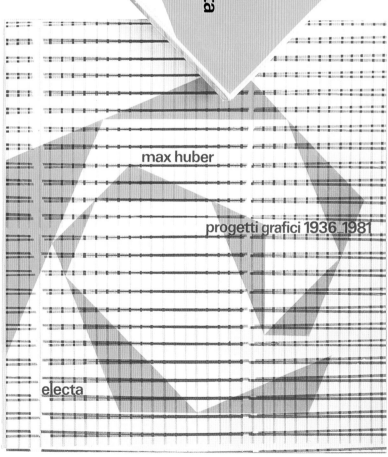

top
La casa rotonda (The Round House)
book cover, Edizioni L'Erba Voglio, 1980
210 x 210 mm

bottom left
Giacometti: sculture, disegni, pitture (Giacometti: Sculpture, drawings and paintings)
poster, Museo Comunale d'Arte Moderna, Ascona, 1985
1280 x 905 mm

bottom centre
Werner Bischof, Paolo Monti
poster, Fotografia oltre, Chiasso, 1983
440 x 630 mm

bottom right
Japan
poster, Museo d'Arte, Mendriso, 1988
1280 x 905 mm

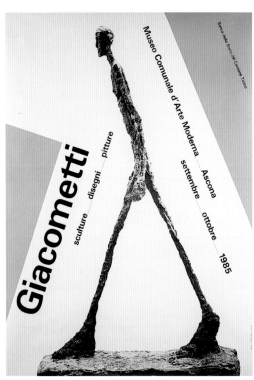

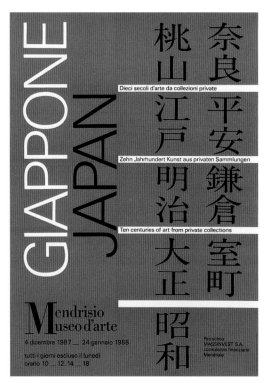

Oskar Schlemmer: un maestro del Bauhaus (Oskar Schlemmer: a Bauhaus Master)
poster, Museo Comunale d'Arte Moderna, Ascona, 1987
1280 x 905 mm

left
Max Huber: Drawings, Paintings, 10 Graphic Works 1936–1940
poster, Top editions Rimoldi, Milan, 1987
700 x 500 mm

top right
Max Huber, Warja Lavater, Otto Teucher
poster, Helmhaus, Zurich, 1990–1
245 x 170 mm

bottom right
Max Huber: grafica 1940-90 (Max Huber: Graphic Design 1940–90)
catalogue cover, Centro Scolastico, Chiasso, 1990
300 x 210 mm

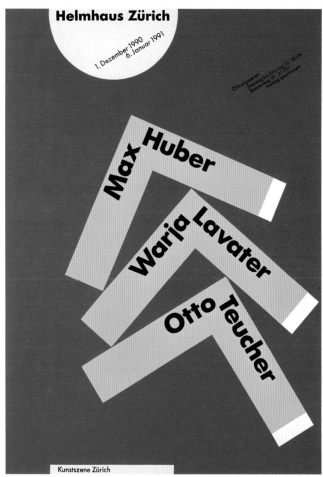

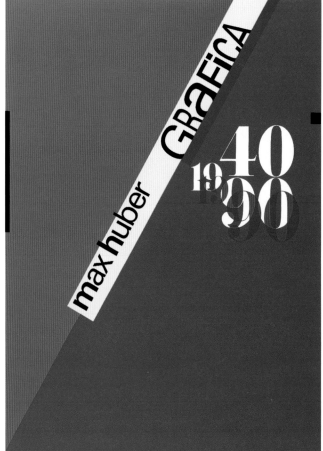

Portfolio: Politics

The historical situation in which Huber found himself during the interwar period, the important contacts he made during his career and the experiences of his friends all made him a natural ally of those fighting in the ranks of the Resistance and, especially after the Second World War, of those propagating the memory of the recent past and the new culture of freedom. Italy had emerged from a long period of ferocious conflict and economic suffering, as well as from a cultural climate that sought to eliminate all differences and multiplicity. Huber, who had been inspired by his early encounters with experimenters and thinkers in Switzerland and later at Studio Boggeri in Milan, saw working for the renewal of society as a major opportunity and applied himself to this within the field of communication. His particular brand of communication became a new social project, subverting the materials and methods of propaganda and elegantly highlighting themes and issues without pomposity or rhetoric. In his work for political organizations, he predominantly used sans serif fonts and silhouetted images, as well as his customary abstract forms and bright colours. Vladimir Tatlin's project for a Monument to the Third International stands out as an oblique structure, where the axis on which the texts are aligned is not the subject in itself; a light structure, it conveys the sense of an ascent and renewal. Huber never conveyed any emotional investment, adopting the designer's characteristic rigour, clearly showing the contribution that the profession could make to a changing society.

**Die Hölle von Maidanek
(The Hell of Maidanek)**
book cover, 1944–5
150 x 105 mm

top
Exposition de la résistance italienne (Italian Resistance Exhibition)
poster, Paris, 1946
700 x 1000 mm

bottom left
Kriegswinterhilfe (Winter War Relief Effort)
study for poster, 1941
160 x 115 mm

bottom right
Arbeiterkulturwoche (Workers' Cultural Week)
poster, Volkshaus, Zurich, 1944
330 x 255 mm

Partito Socialista Ticinese (Ticino Socialist Party)
leaflet cover, 1974
300 x 210 mm

Manifestazione culturale dei comunisti della zona uno (Cultural Demonstration by the Communists from Zone One)
poster, Piazza Mercanti, Milan, 1976
1000 x 700 mm

Sabato 12 giugno 1976 dalle ore 20, in piazza Mercanti, Milano

manifestazione culturale

dei comunisti della zona uno . Milano sezioni del P.C.I.: P. Togliatti, Perotti Devani, Carlo Marx

Video-nastro sulle strutture culturali della zona 1 . Milano e dibattito

Arti figurative

Teatro

Musica

Letture di testi di poesia d'impegno civile

Audiovisivo sulla condizione femminile e dibattito

Mostre sugli attuali problemi politici

Peace Poster
Japan Graphic Designers
Association, Tokyo, 1983
635 x 450 mm

Portfolio: Sport

From 1938, Huber designed posters and flyers for the Monza Races, mainly for the Grand Prix and the Monza Lottery Race. A glance at this series of posters shows the progressive refinement of his visual language. They started with a rigid scan of the field of vision offered by simple bands of colour, superimposed on each other and curved to represent the bends in the track through a modulated perspective. They ended with the use of blurred images produced with an enlarger in the darkroom. Thus Huber built on the suggestion of the perspective of space to achieve the simulation of moving reality.

After the war, the economic recovery brought with it new lifestyles and the dream of fame and wealth that passed into culture via competitions and lotteries. 'Radiotelefortuna', '5000 lire per un sorriso' (5000 Lire for a Smile) – promoted by GiViEmme, the famous Milan perfumer – appeared at the same time as the 'Miss Sorriso' and 'Miss Italia' contests, closely linked to the fledgling Cinecittà, and followed by 'Canzonissima', the celebrated 1970s TV show. The new-found wealth – and available time for leisure and sports such as skiing, golf and tennis, previously the exclusive domain of high society – brought an imagery that was cleverly exploited by the dawning world of advertising.

However, Huber avoided yet again using such persuasion.

Both the magazine Sci (Ski) and the posters for the car races embodied a joyfulness triggered by the combination of primary colours and harmonious lines: the skis were used vertically and photographs were cropped or used in negative, becoming simply oblique additions, lending rhythm to the page and stressing the dynamism of the various sports.

left

**Grosser Preis der Schweiz
(Swiss Grand Prix)**
study for programme cover,
1938
210 x 150 mm

right

**Mille miglia (One
Thousand Miles)**
study for poster, c. 1938
280 x 190 mm

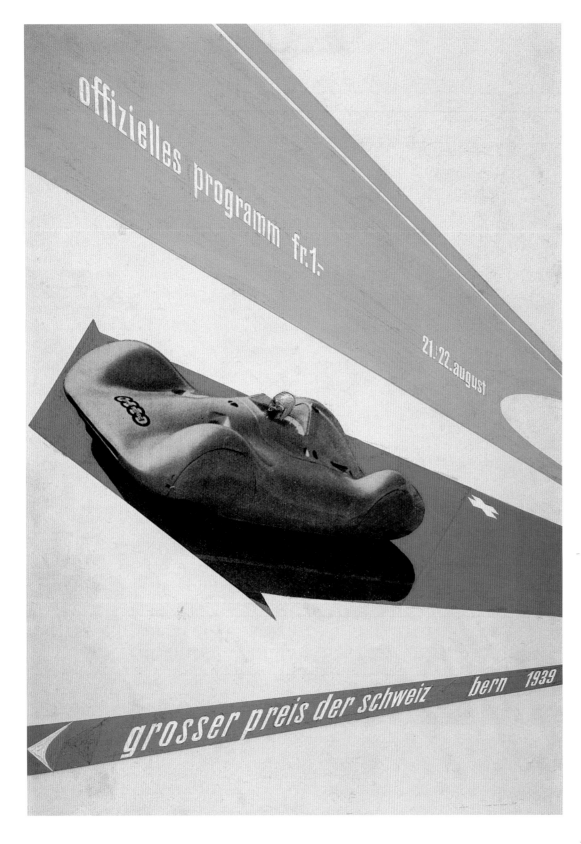

domenica 8 settembre 1968
autodromo di Monza

39° gran premio d'Italia

XXXIX Gran Premio
d'Italia (39th Italian
Grand Prix)
poster, 1968
1000 x 700 mm

left
I Gran Premio della lotteria di Monza (1st Monza Lottery Grand Prix)
poster, 1959
1400 x 1000 mm

right
Italia URSS (Italy USSR)
poster, 1966
1000 x 700 mm

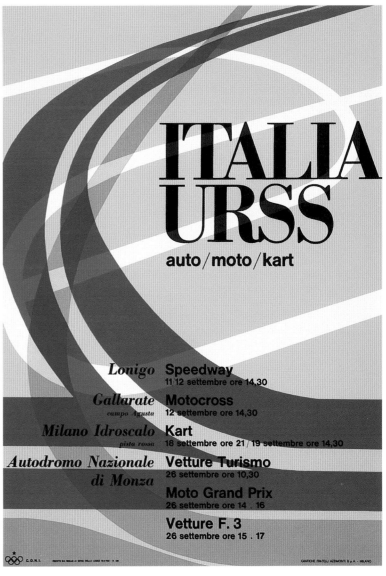

top
**XII Gran Premio della
lotteria di monza
(12th Monza Lottery
Grand Prix)**
preparatory experiments on
photographic paper for
poster, 1970
240 x 300 mm (left)
200 x 280 mm (right)

bottom
**XII Gran Premio della
lotteria di monza
(12th Monza Lottery
Grand Prix)**
poster, 1970
1000 x 700 mm

1000 km di Monza (1000 km of Monza)
poster, 1968
1000 x 700 mm

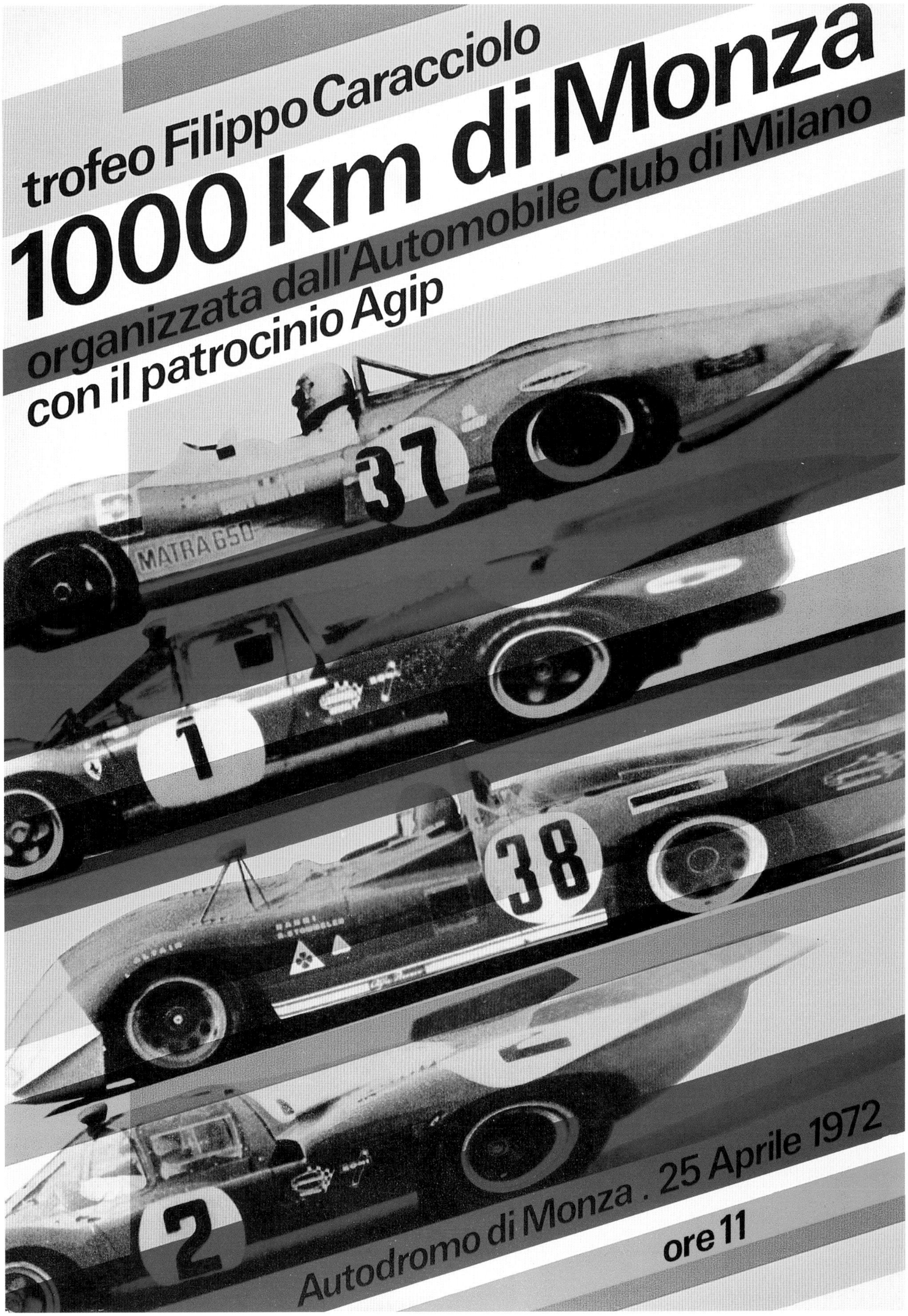

rivista illustrata di sport invernali e di sci nautico - febbraio 1961 - n. 27

left and opposite
Sci (Ski)
magazine covers, 1961–3
275 x 210 mm

rivista illustrata di sport invernali e di sci nautico
marzo 1963 · n. 42

sci

Portfolio: Industry (Early Works)

In the 1950s and 1960s, the Italian economy achieved production levels that have never since been equalled, partly due to relations with the other Western economies. The extraordinary economic boom created family incomes that far exceeded everyday needs. This led to the advent of small cars, electrical appliances, home ownership, package holidays and the manufacture of numerous by-products for the home, office and leisure.

A curious phenomenon of those years was that the pharmaceutical companies invested heavily in communications illustrating the potential of over-the-counter vitamins and medicines in an Italy that had suffered from a shortage of food in the past and that was witnessing the frailty and illness linked to malnutrition. Pharmaceutical companies invested heavily in treatments and tonics, and in cosmetics. Albe Steiner designed for Zamberletti and Bertelli, Remo Muratore for Sifca-Midy, Max Huber for Lepetit and Glaxo. The chemical industry invested in the manufacture of photographic materials – paper and film – with both Steiner and Huber producing a great deal of printed matter and advertisements.

A language based directly on the German avant-garde experience of the 1920s prevailed in Huber's work both for the chemical and pharmaceutical companies and for heavy industry. Silhouetted images of machinery and enlarged pictures of pylons taken from dramatic viewpoints evoked the work of Piet Zwart, just as the repeated use of photgrams lent a symbolic aura to pictures of phials and syringes, going beyond the realism of analogical photography. Once again, Huber transformed mere description into a complex visual language.

riflettete! ...

top left and bottom
Max Huber for Studio
Boggeri
Riflettete! ... (Reflect...!)
leaflet cover and inside
pages, 1940
240 x 145 mm

centre
Max Huber for Studio
Boggeri
CASER
advertisement, 1940
210 x 295 mm

opposite left
Max Huber for Studio
Boggeri
Fotolux
catalogue cover, 1940
210 x 155 mm

opposite right
Max Huber for Studio
Boggeri
Novofotolux
catalogue cover, 1941
205 x 145 mm

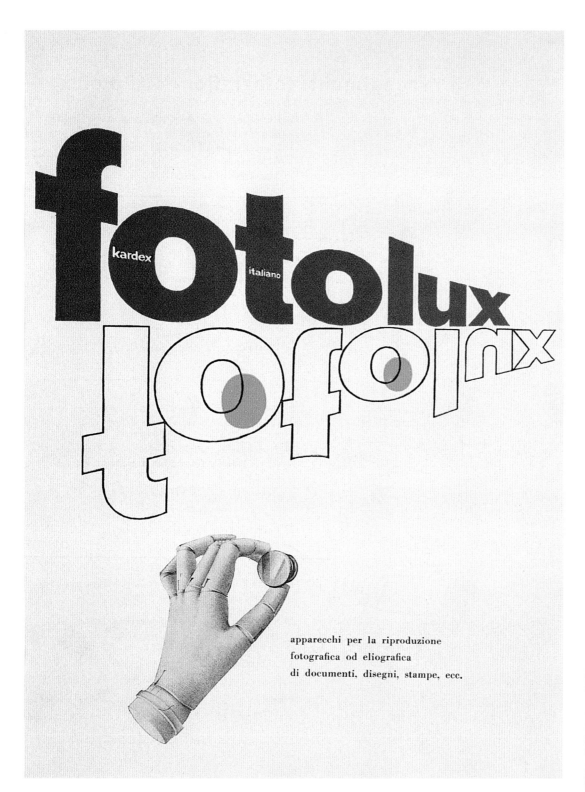

apparecchi per la riproduzione
fotografica od eliografica
di documenti, disegni, stampe, ecc.

Kardex Italiano   novofotolux

milano
corso matteotti 7
tel. 75 238

l'alluminio è prodotto autarchico per eccellenza

lavorazione leghe leggere s.a.
alluminio società anonima

milano · via principe umberto 18-20

alluminio per aeroplani

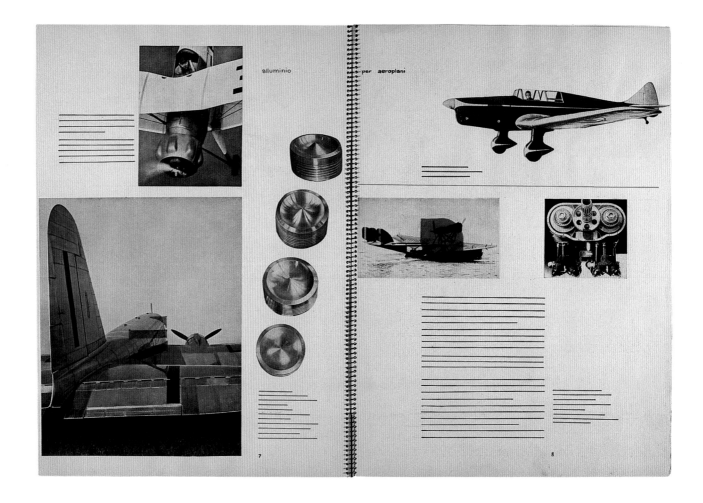

opposite and right
Max Huber for Studio
Boggeri
**Lavorazione Leghe
Leggere (Manufacture of
Light Aluminium Alloy)**
study for brochure, 1940
430 x 295 mm

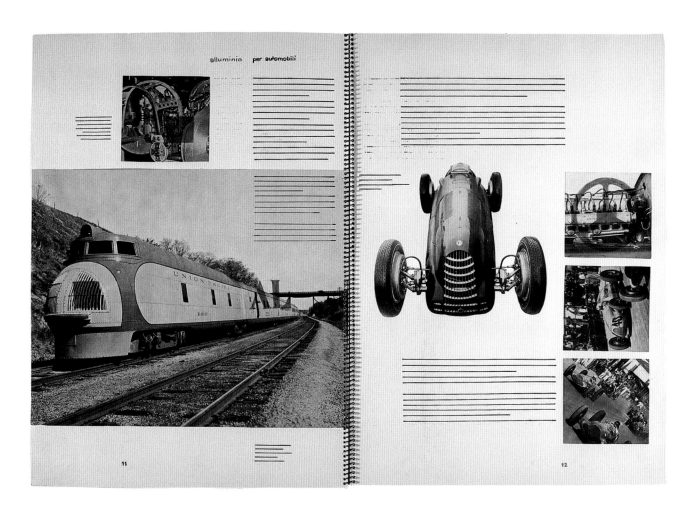

**Per l'autarchia
(For Economic Self-suffi-
cency)**
advertisement, 1940
330 x 235 mm

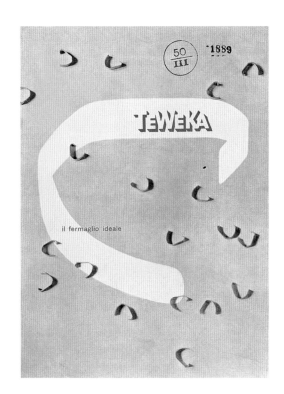

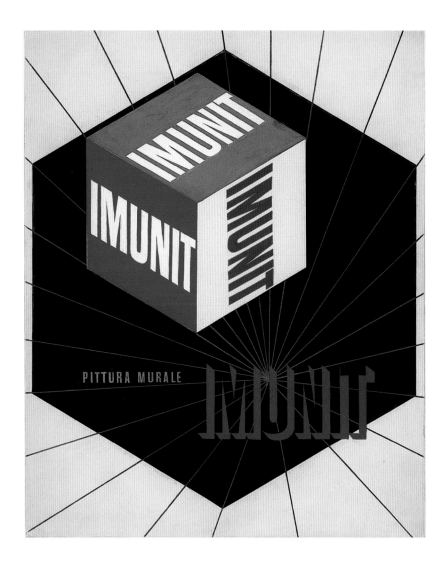

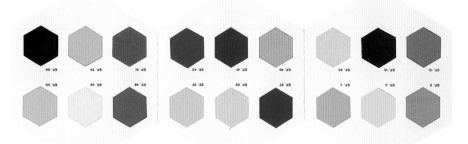

top
Max Huber for Studio
Boggeri
Imunit
poster, 1940
295 x 240 mm

bottom
Max Huber for Studio
Boggeri
Imunit
leaflet, 1940
155 x 130 mm

opposite top left
Max Huber for Studio
Boggeri
Glaxo
leaflet cover, 1940
205 x 120 mm

opposite top right
Max Huber for Studio
Boggeri
Glaxo
advertisement, 1940
200 x 130 mm

opposite bottom
Max Huber for Studio
Boggeri
Glaxo
advertisement, 1940
220 x 160 mm

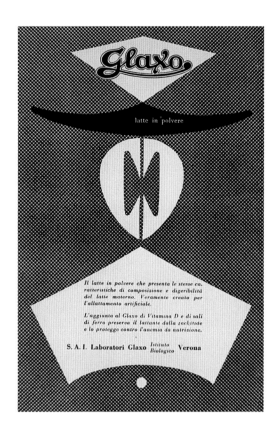

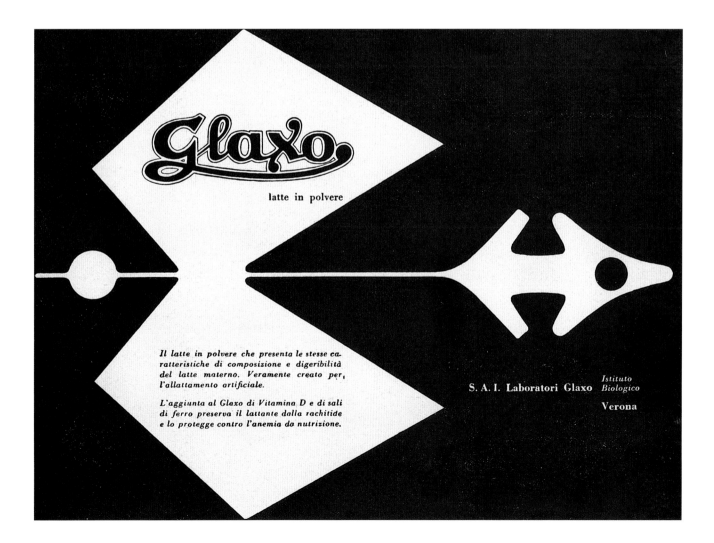

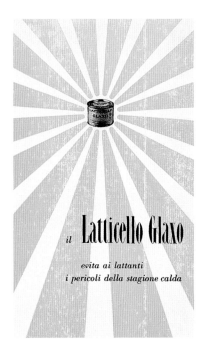

il **Latticello Glaxo**

*evita ai lattanti
i pericoli della stagione calda*

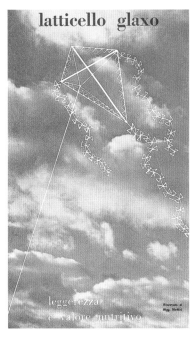

latticello glaxo

*leggerezza
e valore nutritivo*

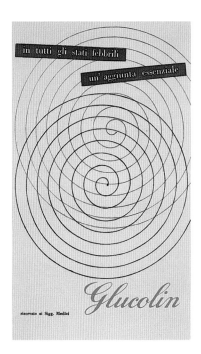

in tutti gli stati febbrili
un' aggiunta essenziale

Glucolin

riservato ai Sigg. Medici

riservato ai Sigg. Medici

glucolin

reintegratore delle forze durante la stagione estiva

opposite left
Max Huber for Studio
Boggeri
**Latticello Glaxo (Glaxo
Buttermilk)**
leaflet cover, 1940
210 x 125 mm

opposite right
Max Huber for Studio
Boggeri
Ostelin Glaxo
leaflet cover, 1940
210 x 120 mm

top left
Max Huber for Studio
Boggeri
**Latticello Glaxo (Glaxo
Buttermilk)**
leaflet cover, 1940
210 x 120 mm

top centre left
Max Huber for Studio
Boggeri
**Latticello Glaxo (Glaxo
Buttermilk)**
leaflet cover, 1940
205 x 12 mm

top centre right and top
right
Max Huber for Studio
Boggeri
Glucolin Glaxo
leaflet covers, 1940,
210 x 125 mm

bottom
Max Huber for Studio
Boggeri
Glucolin Glaxo
leaflet, 1940
205 x 240 mm

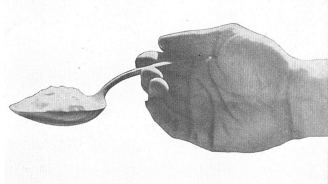

GLUCOLIN

Destrosio monoidr.	gr. 9,80
Calcio glicerof.	» 0,10
Olio arach. idrog.	» 0,007
Vit. D (calciferolo)	90 U. I.

Nelle acidosi, stati febbrili, ma-
lattie cardiache, disordini epati-
ci, cure pre . e post-operatorie,
debilità degli adulti, affaticamen-
to e anoressia.

Le dosi saranno stabilite secondo
la necessità partendo da un mi-
nimo di 50 gr.

S. A. I. LABORATORI GLAXO **GL** *Istituto Biologico* VERONA

Glucolin
e cure termali

Riservato ai Sigg. Medici

CMS 18500 - 0640 - Aut. Pref. N. 14801 del 24-5-39-XVII - STUDIO BOGGERI S.A. - Tip. A. Lucini & C.

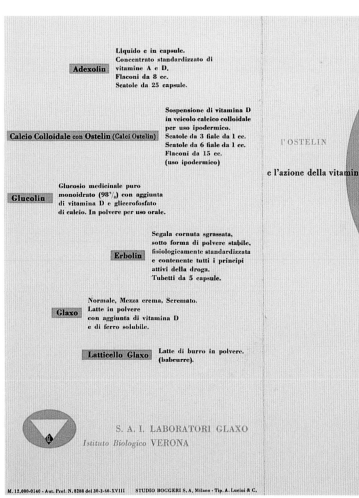

top
Max Huber for Studio
Boggeri
Ostelin Glaxo
catalogue cover, 1940
230 x 210 mm

bottom left
Max Huber for Studio
Boggeri
Ostelin Glaxo
catalogue cover, 1940
120 x 210 mm

bottom right
Max Huber for Studio
Boggeri
Ostelin Glaxo
catalogue cover, 1940
210 x 125 mm

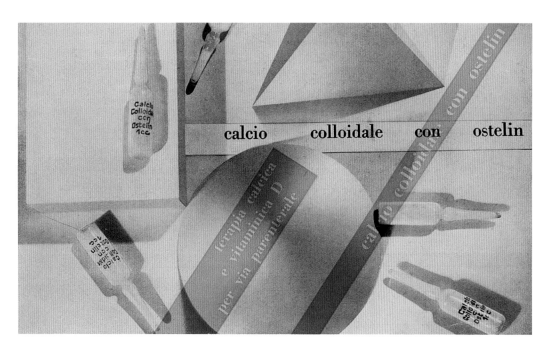

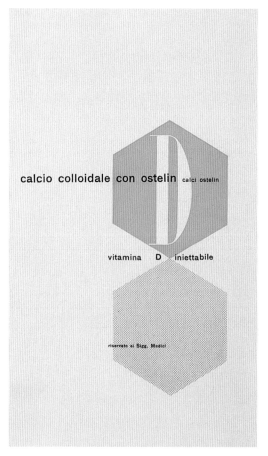

Max Huber for Studio
Boggeri
**Latticello Glaxo (Glaxo
Buttermilk)**
catalogue cover, 1940
250 x 125 mm

primi calori........

primi disturbi della nutrizione

perchè dovete preferire il

Glaxo

Con il LATTICELLO GLAXO, latticello fresco in polvere, è possibile rieducare l'intestino del lattante dopo una diarrea dovuta al caldo e ritornare all'alimentazione normale. Oltre che come alimento curativo trova precise indicazioni in tutti quei disordini della nutrizione dovuti alle irrazionali alimentazioni spesso seguite dalle madri.

S. A. I. LABORATORI GLAXO Istituto Biologico VERONA

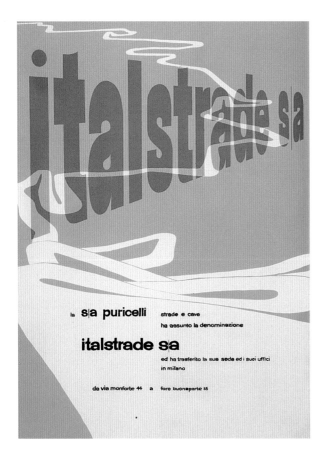

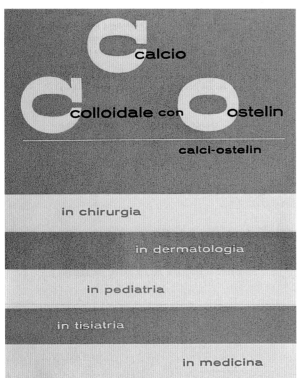

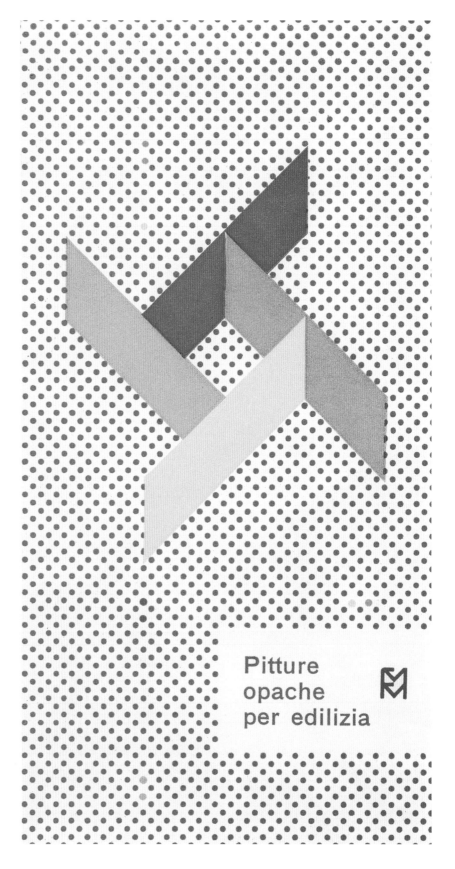

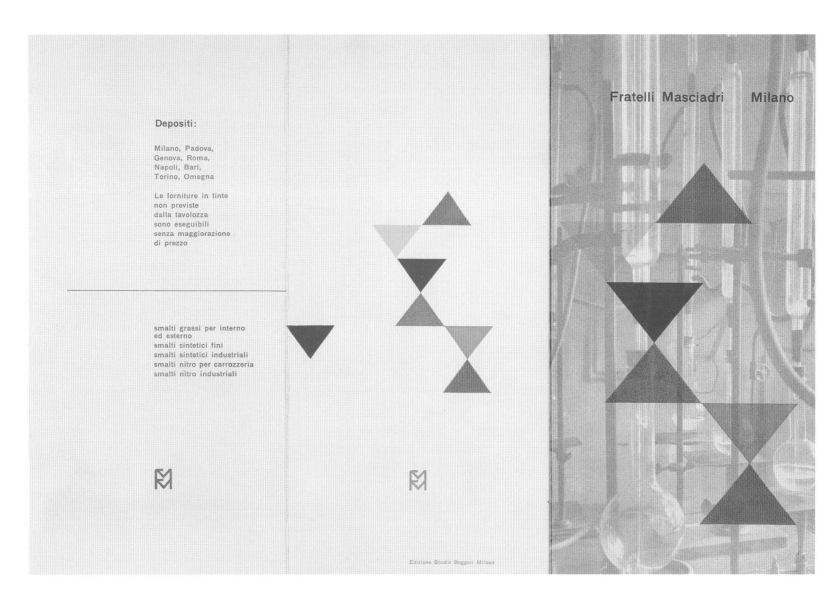

2

The Milan Years

Stanislaus von Moos

Half a century after they were commissioned, many of Max Huber's visual communication designs are still being used by companies and supermarket chains today. They are an ongoing part of our everyday lives and provide a legacy of standard references. The best-known examples are the trademark and logo of the La Rinascente department store in Milan, which Huber designed in 1950, the trademark of the COIN clothing and household goods store, designed in 1955 and the Esselunga logo, created in 1958 for the Supermarket chain.

Huber's projects and all the associated research and design material – sketeches, trials and variations – are safeguarded in archives made public on the initiative of his widow, Aoi Kono, after she created the Fondazione Max Huber.Kono with the m.a.x. Museo in Chiasso, Switzerland. Amongst the few European archives of twentieth-century communication, they immediately became a valuable resource for enthusiasts and scholars. The material illustrates the time span between the late 1930s and the 1980s. It tells of the post-war years, the premises on which contemporary society built its visual imagery, the changes that occurred during the 1950s and 1960s and the difficult years of the 1970s. Consulting these archives is a sociological experience that goes beyond one designer's famous projects. The documents clearly show that the collective visual experience in Italy has passed through a filter created by Huber. In many cases, the objects and products he helped advertise may have been forgotten, but his presentations live on.

Huber started working in 1936 at the age of seventeen, having studied at the Kunstgewerbeschule Zürich (Zurich School of Arts and Crafts). After coming into contact with his contemporary masters, both through direct acquaintance – Max Bill, Hans Neuburg, Josef Müller-Brockmann – and through their works – El Lissitzky and László Moholy-Nagy among others – he started seeking new interlocutors. In 1940, at the age of twenty-one, he began working at Studio Boggeri in Milan, a crossroads on the international design scene, where many of the brightest young Italian, Swiss and German practitioners were already working.[1] Despite his youth, he immediately began to impose his creative talent, thanks partly to the valuable lessons he had learnt from his teacher at the Kunstgewerbeschule, the photographer and experimenter Alfred Willimann.

Antonio Boggeri had opened his studio in 1933 and it would continue until 1981, with Boggeri as its sole proprietor and art director. He had originally studied violin at the Conservatory in Milan (he and Huber shared a love of music from the beginning of their association), but received 'in the field' training from 1924 to 1932 as Director of Alfieri & Lacroix, Milan's leading printer. Here, he came into contact with publications designed by Jan Tschichold, Moholy-Nagy, El Lissitzky and others. This contact with the work of the best international designers prompted him to seek young collaborators with an international background when he opened his studio in 1933. In 1932, at the 5th Milan Triennale, he came across the work of Imre Reiner, whom he employed alongside Kate Bernhardt, and in 1934, he started working with Xanti Schawinsky, who was responsible for initiating a renewal of visual languages in Italy thanks to his expertise in the technical methods he had learnt at the Bauhaus.

During the early part of the century, the Bauhaus had been responsible for the huge advances made in disciplines such as photography and product design. Through investigations and analysis in this sphere, it had defined for the first time the specifics of disciplines previously considered minor due to the fact that they were produced by mechanical means. After the school was finally closed by the Nazis in 1933, the dispersal of its students across Europe (Switzerland, France and Italy in particular) offered a major opportunity for the dissemination of the new design culture. The former Bauhaus students working for Studio Boggeri – Reiner, Bernhardt and Schawinsky – passed on methods that fascinated the other young assistants and legitimized the instincts and practices of many artists and designers already active in Italy, with profound consequences for design and photography.

Schawinsky's work was particularly crucial because of the photographic experiments he had conducted in the years spent at the Bauhaus. He had analyzed and recognized, for example, the expressive value of the screen, a regular, abstract filter placed between image and lens. This was only one sphere in an investigation that explored specific techniques and drew on elements that would lead beyond the pictorial phase of photography. The use of the screen, which helped reveal the ambiguity of photographic realism, gained added significance when it was replaced by the enlarged half-tone screen, which evidenced the nature of the technique employed to produce the printed work. Schawinsky also highlighted other factors that distinguished experimental German photography: a distorted perspective created by bring-

Max Huber

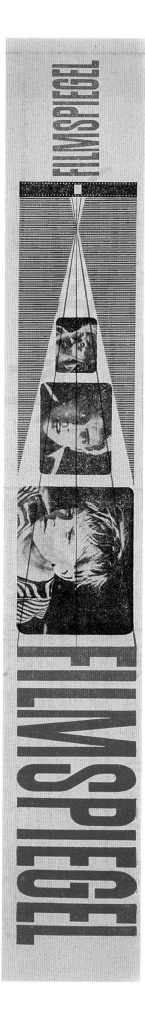

FILMSPIEGEL

opposite
Max Huber
self-portrait, 1940

Filmspiegel
newspaper section
masthead, 1943
295 x 45 mm

ing the lens close to the object, the use of the shadow as a subject, the study of exposure times and the effects of over-exposure on light-sensitive paper, a love of 'non-photogenic' subjects (mechanisms, springs), different angles (from above, skimming the surface, tilted, close-up), and the subjective shot. Schawinsky had learnt how to achieve a new complexity of observation and this spread immediately from the field of research to the professional world.

Schawinsky's experiences influenced all those working at Studio Boggeri, and experiments with photograms and cut-outs, as in Herbert Bayer's photomontages, fuelled their research: Franco Grignani, Omar Calabrese, Giovanni Pintori, Albe Steiner and many others worked enthusiastically in this field. In the early part of the century, Anton Giulio Bragaglia's photographic experimentation, under the auspices of the Italian Futurist movement,[2] had already shown how visual disciplines could intersect, and that the traditionally analogical rendition of reality had already become a thing of the past. Carlo Bertelli wrote of the young Italian researchers of the 1930s (Luigi Veronesi, Grignani, Steiner, Marcello Nizzoli, Remo Muratore): 'Not only did the whole old debate … on the rivalry between photography and painting go out the door, but a whole new contamination between photography and painting emerged in Italy.'[3] In 1956 Veronesi added in *Ferrania*:

> an exposure is not a real photograph, it merely records the form, transparency and shadows of an object. The image obtained is never a document, but the transformation of an object into a pure play of light and shadow … in most cases, the picture comes within that 'metaphysical' or 'abstract' approach that has influenced and conditioned much European art.[4]

During the second half of the 1930s, Studio Boggeri became the focal point for the young people who were actively engaged in redefining work that had previously been carried out by artists, architects, illustrators and printers in Italy. From that time on, they clearly saw that the challenge was in overcoming aesthetic tyranny and lending legitimacy and authority to the profession of graphic design. Carlo Bertelli, for instance, stated that: 'basically this Italian avant-garde is an avant-garde of applied art'.[5]

Following his technical training, Huber sensed a need to lend purpose and meaning to his already highly developed skills. The typography and photography he had learnt as a student in Zurich (he was on the same course as the photographer Werner Bishof) were to be turned, in Milan, into visual communication, and assumed a value that would transform aesthetics into ethics, serving to convey a clear message. He saw Milan in general and Studio Boggeri in particular as the melting pot in which illustration, painting, photography and printing could come together, with graphic design – a developing discipline – synthesizing them all.

At this time in Italy's history, comparisons with international experience were not possible because of a presumed cultural self-sufficiency. British and American literature, abstract art and jazz music, for example, were considered degenerate manifestations of the noble arts. The highly unusual situation at Studio Boggeri, however, based on Boggeri's refined tastes and international outlook – he was already in contact with Bayer, Marcel Breuer and Walter Gropius by 1935 – provided Huber with the opportunity to exchange ideas with other enthusiasts of his own age. Not only did he come into contact with leading exponents in the field of graphic design but also with avant-garde artists and intellectuals. He was no longer a pupil but a major player in a new wave that seemed to be unstoppable.

At the outbreak of the Second World War, Huber was forced to return to Switzerland. Between 1942 and 1944, during this brief return to his homeland, he spent time with the members of Allianz Vereiningung moderner Schweizer Künstler (Alliance, the Association of Modern Swiss Artists) in Zurich. In 1942,

he participated in the exhibition 'Abstrakt Konkret' at the Kunsthaus. But he had found Studio Boggeri and the Milanese context so stimulating that he returned there as soon as possible, crossing the border at Vacallo, near Como, on foot and without a visa.

On his return in 1945, he became perhaps Boggeri's most influential assistant, helping to establish the Studio's style. Dozens of creative people passed through the Studio, contributing to its success and to Huber's intellectual growth: Ezio Bonini, Aldo Calabresi, Erberto Carboni, Fortunato de Pero, Adolf Fluckinger, Grignani, Giancarlo Iliprandi, Lora Lamm, Arnaud Maggs, Enzo Mari, Armando Milani, Bruno Monguzzi, Bruno Munari, Muratore, Till Neuburg, Nizzoli, Bob Noorda, Hazy Osterwalder, Riccardo Ricas, Roberto Sambonet, Saul Steinberg, Steiner, Carlo Vivarelli, Heinz Waibl and more. Some of these figures produced a number of famous publications for the Studio, including *foto-tipo* (Boggeri and Huber), *Dimensioni* (with architects Gian Luigi Banfi, Lodovico Barbiano di Belgiojoso and Enrico Peresutti), *Tipografia-Arte costruttiva-Architettura* and *Foto–tipo–grafica* (both with Max Bill) – all crucial to the debate about design culture in Italy. At the request of Gio Ponti, they also redesigned the architectural journal *Domus*, which, with its new graphic format, became one of the leading international architecture and design journals.[6]

The most crucial contact that Huber made while working for Studio Boggeri was with Albe Steiner. Steiner introduced Huber to his world and together they entered into a personal and professional association that was to last a lifetime. Steiner came from a middle-class Milanese family and developed a commitment to anti-Fascism when his uncle, Giacomo Matteotti, was assassinated by the Fascist regime in 1924. This resulted in his involvement in the Resistance in Val d'Ossola, where he served as political

above
Arte astratta e concreta (Abstract and Concrete Art)
view of exhibition, Palazzo Reale, Milan, 1947

bottom left
Allianz Exhibition
study for poster, Kunsthaus Zurich, 1942
160 x 111 mm

bottom right
Abstrakt Konkret (Abstract Concrete)
magazine cover, Galerie des Eaux Vives, Zurich, 1946
300 x 210 mm

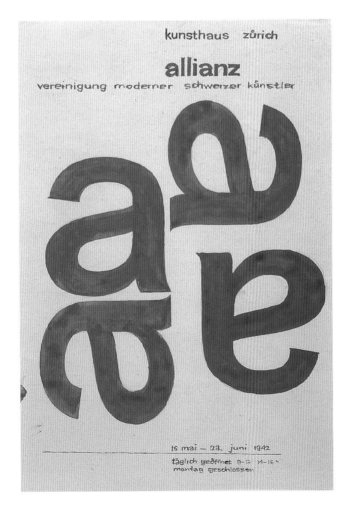

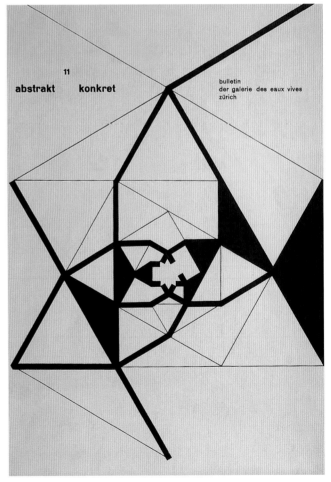

Arte astratta e concreta
(Abstract and Concrete
Art)
poster, Palazzo Reale,
Milan, 1947
1000 x 700 mm

left
Fiesta
book cover, Einaudi, 1946
195 x 130 mm

right
Einaudi
advertisement, 1947
150 x 100 mm

commissioner of the 85th Brigata Garibaldi. In 1933 he started working as a graphic designer. He and his wife Lica were close to the Communist Party in 1939 and he became involved in the underground press with Elio Vittorini. After the Liberation, he was asked to prepare the layout of *Il Politecnico* (The Polytechnic), which published its first issue in September 1945; he also worked for the Turin-based publishing house Einaudi, set up by Giulio, the son of Luigi Einaudi, first President of the fledgling Republic. He involved Huber in this project as well as in his work on the series Biblioteca del Politecnico (Polytechnic Library) and a whole range of political publications. In the publishing sector, he worked at length with the publishers Giangiacomo Feltrinelli, Vangelista and Zanichelli, and the Communist Party. He laid out many photographic, graphic design and architectural journals, as well as a large number of cultural publications. He enjoyed countless professional relationships with companies such as Bemberg, Aurora, RAI, Bertelli, Geigy, Pierrel, and was involved in and designed both cultural and commercial exhibitions at the Fiera di Milano (Milan Trade Fair) and the Milan Triennale. In 1973 he created the design and publications for the Memorial and Museum of Political and Racial Deportees in Carpi di Modena for ANED – (Associazione Nazionale Ex Deportati - National Association of Former Deportees) – and remained a prominent figure in Italy until his death in 1974. In 1977, Huber (along with Lica and the Steiners' daughter Anna) laid out the catalogue for an exhibition of his work held at Castello Sforzesco in Milan, in a last gesture of his esteem.

Huber saw Steiner as an inspirational figure. The quality of his projects and his clear vision of the role of designer – no longer as an executor, but as a protagonist – made him a highly original figure on the Italian scene. He, more than others, argued strongly that the job of graphic artist must be seen as a key activity in the cultural sphere. Together, these two significant designers formed a bond based on their complementary characters and skills, as well as their mutual esteem. They belonged to the generation of change – not just political and social, but above all, cultural. Both were the creators of a new professional identity and they intended to pass this on to others. Today their alliance allows for an appraisal of the differences and similarities not only in their own work, but also, more generally, in the Swiss school that was born out of the avant-gardes. Their ideas challenged the nineteenth-century approach and redefined the Italian school, which had been accustomed to an analogical relationship with reality but, thanks to the Studio Boggeri

experience and Steiner's febrile activity, now began moving along the path of designer awareness and responsibility.

In 1946 Steiner moved to Mexico in order to work with Hannes Meyer on a literacy campaign and on the Taller de Gráfica Popular (Workshop of Popular Graphics) with Diego Rivera, Alfaro Siqueiros, Leopoldo Mendes and others. He asked Huber to take over the work he had begun on the 8th Milan Triennale. In the same year, Huber moved temporarily into Einaudi's Milan offices, on viale Tunisia. He slept on a camp bed and worked non stop, creating book covers and layouts. Living and working in the same space, often toiling late into the night and sleeping beside his design table so as not to waste any time, shows the uninterrupted continuity between his life and profession.

Huber always worked on a freelance basis and consistently collaborated directly with each client. This indicates an autonomous approach that favoured direct relationships born out of shared esteem and equal intentions. These exchanges with different clients, and their briefs, as well as the daily challenge of the graphic designer's job – typographies, inks and grids – provided Huber with the opportunity to combine various elements, including photography, in his search for a new syntax.

In an interview, Huber recalled that after the war, materials – including paper – were in short supply, and that Einaudi had borrowed money from him to pay the printer for *Il Politecnico*; the loan was repaid, of course. It seems surprising that anyone should have wanted to be in Milan in such difficult times but it appears that the enthusiasm and opportunity for stimulating encounters with international colleagues were enough to make up for it. Einaudi was an inspiration for Italian intellectuals, and Milan was the hub of Italy's theatre and music culture, as well as of its economic rebirth; the Milan Triennale and the Fiera di Milano gave it an international presence. Huber received the Gold Medal of the 8th Milan Triennale in 1947, on which he worked first with Steiner and then with the architect Piero Bottoni.

A greater understanding of the complexity of that chequered post-war period in Milan is aided by the recollections of Roberto Leydi, a music historian and Huber's lifelong friend and professional accomplice. He paints an affectionate and precise picture of the irrepressible longing for cultural reconstruction at that time. In a text dating from the early 1990s he recalls:

The houses were still in ruins, the streets destroyed, and services uncertain; everything had to be rebuilt and, above all, recreated; we didn't have the bare necessities for survival. Yet, in such a situation, which should have pushed all cultural projects way back, Milan came up with Nando Ballo's [orchestra] I Pomeriggi Musicali, Paolo Grassi and Giorgio Strehler's [independent theatre] Piccolo Teatro, Elio Vittorini's [magazine] *Il Politecnico*, the publisher Rosa e Ballo, the renewal movements of the young painters of Oltre Guernica and the formation of the movement Arte Astratta e Concreta [Abstract and Concrete Art], architects' ideas and projects (and their execution), the spreading of industrial and graphic design, and the ferment of musical research that, with Luciano Berio, led shortly afterwards to the creation of the RAI recording studio …. Giorgio Strehler said later about the creation of the Piccolo Teatro that he and Paolo Grassi managed to give rise to that institution because, in the fired climate of the times, they did not realise that it was an impossible and perhaps blasphemous dream to want to build a new theatre in a city where there was no milk for the children, where the debris formed a catastrophic cityscape and where the trams were just starting to run again.[7]

The 1950s and 1960s were years full of energy for Huber, released through exciting encounters with architects and designers but also with musicians, artists, poets and writers both in Italy and abroad. These contacts were to have a crucial impact on his professional career. In 1950 he made his first trip to Paris, where he met the artists Georges Vantongerloo and Alberto Giacometti. He also exhibited at the exhibition '20 European Designers' at the University of California in Los Angeles. At the 9th Milan Triennale he was awarded the Compasso d'oro for textile design and worked with the architects Belgiojoso, Peressutti and Ernesto Rogers on the design of the section 'La forma dell'utile' (The Shape of Useful Things). He met Herbert Bayer, a former teacher at the Bauhaus in Dessau.

From 1950 to 1954, Huber worked for the department store La Rinascente as art director of the advertising office, where he was in charge of interior and exterior designs. Opened in Milan in 1877 by the Bocconi brothers with the name Aux villes d'Italie, the shop was re-christened in 1918 by Gabriele d'Annunzio. After the Second World War, with the growth in mass consumption, La Rinascente renovated its interiors and sales organization, entrusting its visual identity to Huber. Thanks to the presence of Steiner as advertising art director and of the internal communication coordinator Carlo Pagani, in 1954 La Rinascente promoted the 'Compasso d'oro – Per l'estetica del prodotto' award, following an exhibition on the aesthetic qualities of everyday objects. In 1959, this award came under the aegis of ADI (Associazione per il Disegno Industriale – Industrial Design Association) founded in 1956, and is still one of the most coveted design awards.

In the period 1955 to 1956, in Milan, Huber met Leo Lionni, who promoted the publication of the works already produced by Huber for the American journal *Print.* This was also the time when he started working with the brothers Achille and Pier Giacomo Castiglioni on the 'Mostra internazionale del petrolio' (International Oil Exhibition) in Bari and for the ENI (Ente Nazionale Idrocarburi – National Oil Organization) pavilion at the Fiera di Milano, a professional relationship that was to continue for decades, in Italy and abroad.

During these years, photography was being used on a massive scale to advertise industrial products, whose appealing form and function could only be conveyed by a new, perspicuous photographer's eye. In Italy, it was not the photographers but the young graphic designers who were excelling in this field, producing images of products to be used in conjunction with text in advertisements, posters and brochures. Both the innate nature of photography – the technique adopted to produce the picture – and that of typography – the technique adopted to produce printed matter – became objects of research. Applied arts – photography, printing, manufactured furnishings,

right
Max Huber at the Compasso d'oro award ceremony
1954

bottom left
La Rinascente: Compasso d'oro 1955
brochure cover, 1955
215 x 430 mm

bottom right
Premio la Rinascente Compasso d'oro 1956 (La Rinascente-Compasso d'oro Award 1956)
poster, Circolo della Stampa, Milan, 1956
700 x 1000 mm

compasso d'oro 1955

Max Huber   intrasoceus - manfesto numero 3 della cartella - 8 stampo- este nell'ottobre 1987 de Paolo dalmicch e Roberto Gozzi

graphic design and visual communication as well as product design – were the new disciplines in a post-war Milan that was busily in search of economic reconstruction.

This was confirmed by the foundation of the school Convitto Scuola Rinascita, made possible by cooperation between ANPI (Associazione Nazionale Partigiani Italiani – Italian National Partisan Association) and the Ministry for Post-War Assistance, whose aim was to reintroduce those who had fought in the war to the professional world. Huber, Steiner, Muratore and Veronesi, as well as Gabriele Mucchi, were appointed as teachers on the first graphic design course. It was an experimental venture, a sort of proto-didactics involving five teachers and five students. It did not have a clear educational programme or method at this time; rather, the aim was to create a workshop where teachers and students collaborated actively on real professional contracts, sharing responsibilities and credit equally. The Albe e Lica Steiner Archive in Milan contains meeting minutes and material on its aims and methods but no subject syllabuses; every teacher passed on his or her personal experience and knowledge. Huber taught type design and how to control projects at the printing phase. The proceeds from the works produced were reinvested in the activities of the Convitto and used to purchase materials and to support the students.

The Rinascita experience lasted for many years but some of the central figures soon branched out in independent professional directions. Both Mucchi and Veronesi returned to strictly artistic activities, the one to the world of painting and sculpture, moving to East Berlin, the other to that of experimentation and abstract art. Huber, Muratore and Steiner, meanwhile, fully embraced their design careers.

Since the early twentieth century, the city of Milan had been the home of Italy's most international professional school, the Scuola del Libro, which formed part of the educational project of the Società Umanitaria. This society was founded in the late nineteenth century following a substantial bequest from Moisè Loria, a wealthy entrepreneur, to the City of Milan. His donation was for the creation of a free school, organised to enable the less well off 'to emancipate themselves'.

In the two or three years before the courses began, the school's directors prepared a study of employment levels in the area, as well as the main types of production and the latest European teaching methods. The British Arts and Crafts movement was its most significant model, and life drawing as well as the study of materials (wood, metal, glass), were presented as the starting points for a reflection on nature, the template for every possible human project.

Analysis of Lombardy's main production in the last two decades of the nineteenth century showed that a large percentage of the economic resources had been put into publishing and journalism; there was thus a pressing need for skilled workers in printing and all the processes leading up to it. The school Scuola Professionale di Tipografia in Milan had been opened in 1886 by various typographical associations and was absorbed by the Scuola del Libro of the Società Umanitaria on 13 March 1904.

When Steiner was appointed Director of the Scuola del Libro in 1959, the courses already had a fifty-year history and had won widespread international recognition. Steiner's direction, from 1959 until his death, was a crucial turning point for the Scuola del Libro, which passed from the noblest printing and bookbinding tradition to a new phase. Steiner replaced Michele Provinciali who, after a crucial period at the New Bauhaus in Chicago, had started the first photography courses in 1954.

The Scuola del Libro became more complex after the introduction of photography, no longer practised for its photomechanical function, serving printing and lithography, but as a discipline in its own right. Its purpose was to produce pictures of objects, portraits and landscapes that would illustrate the world, but also to create printed material, advertisements and posters. Both the type of photography that borrowed from the German experiences of the 1920s and the more pragmatic one stemming from the American Sraight Photography movement, were taught as well as more experimental approaches.

This brought the introduction of graphic design courses, with a more precise teaching structure than had been seen in the past. The skills needed to organize the visual field – grids, golden section, etc. – were defined, as well as the study of lettering. The theory of colour, developed by Johannes Itten at the Bauhaus, was also taught along with printing techniques and psychology of perception. Milan's leading creators, graphic artists and photographers took turns at teaching in those years; Huber gave courses on lettering and design.

His graphics at this time were constantly reaching out in a search for mediation between the experimental and the specifics of the commission. In his series of posters commenced in 1958 for automobile events, mainly at the Monza motor-racing track, he worked on variations in the depth of field, never using images in the strict sense but mixing unframed subjects with strips of colour to convey dynamism and speed. He employed visual prompts and played with the imagery, but never imposed literal descriptions. These images extended beyond the Italian tradition, in which illustration had been the major protagonist.

In the late 1950s Huber started working with Nava Arti Grafiche, one of the leading printing firms in Milan. This enabled him to continue concentrating on lettering and typography, the bases of his training, although he also worked on countless other jobs. His research and experimentation found an outlet for expression thanks to his ability to push the technical limits of his designs. Felice Nava commissioned the leading graphic designers of the day to create his calendars, diaries and office materials, often working with Boggeri. His products ushered in a period of innovation onto the Italian scene, generating new design theories and allowing designers to develop their skills through experimentation with the most advanced techniques and technologies. To this day, the designs made during this period remain some of the most interesting ever produced.

By this time Milan, was becoming the link between Italy and international culture, and Huber was a leading player. His international career took off between 1957 and 1958. The Type Directors Club in New York invited him to speak at the first International Seminar of Typography, held in Silvermine, Connecticut, where he met Otl Aicher, Will Burtin, Yusaku Kamekura, the writer Bruce MacKenzie and other intellectuals. During his first visit to the United States, he went to Boston, encountering Gyorgy Kepes and Walter Gropius at MIT, and to Chicago, where he visited the Institute of Design, the Teobald

Olivetti
brochure cover and inside
pages, 1957
210 x 240 mm

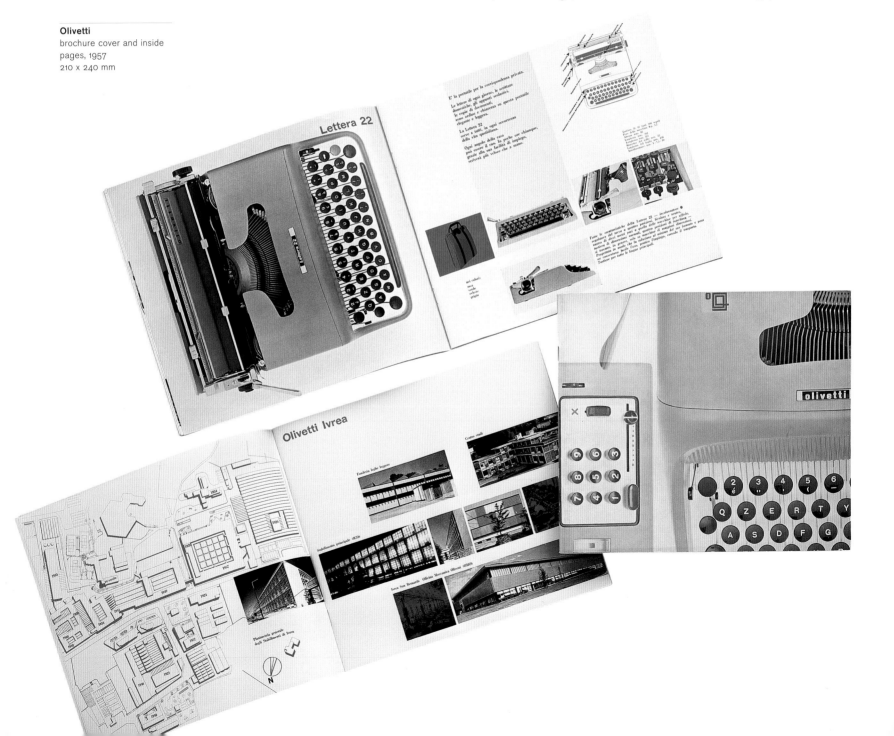

right
**Felice Nava and
Max Huber at the
opening of an exhibition
of Max Huber's paintings**
Galleria Mosaico, Chiasso,
1971

left
1964 Calendar
Nicola Moneta, 1964
160 x 130 mm

publishing house and the Ludlow Type foundry. In Italy, he worked with the writer Giorgio Soavi on the photographic book *50 anni Olivetti* (Olivetti Fifty Years), which saw the participation of internationally acclaimed photographers including Ugo Mulas and Emil Schulthess. He and Soavi visited the School in Ulm and learnt about the Dutch design scene. In 1959, he started teaching on the graphic design courses of the Società Umanitaria in Milan and returned to the United States on a trip organized by the Architects' Association of Milan, where he met Paul Rand, Lester Beall, Aaron Burns – a type-design theoretician – Marcel Breuer and others.

The international situation favoured cultural exchanges and this opening up of borders permitted relationships that produced profitable ventures. In 1960, Huber organized from Milan the exhibition '10 Milan Designers' at The Composing Room's Gallery 303 in New York, with works by Boggeri, Carboni, Grignani, Munari, Noorda, Pintori, Provinciali, Steiner and Waibl. In 1960, he was also invited to speak at the World Design Conference in Tokyo, which he attended with Munari. His frequent international trips brought him into contact with other major graphic designers, both American and Japanese, as well as with architects, including Buckminster Fuller, Kenzo Tange and Katzki Iwabuki.

In 1961, AGI (Alliance Graphique International) organized a conference in Milan and Huber and Pintori designed the exhibition of international graphics in the Contemporary Art Pavilion. On that occasion, Saul Bass, Anton Stankowski, Walter Herdeg and one of Japan's leading graphic designers, Takashi Kono, with his daughter Aoi – an illustrator who was studying at the Konstfackskolan in Stockholm – all came to Milan. Huber went to Stockholm and returned with Aoi. He rented an apartment in Morbio Inferiore, in Ticino, Switzerland, and married her.

During 1962 and 1963, he continued working on exhibition designs with the Castiglioni brothers. At the subsequent AGI exhibition in Amsterdam, Huber showed several projects, including many executed for Nava. In the same years, he exhibited at Documenta in Kassel and travelled at length with Aoi in southern Italy. Between 1964 and 1965, he and Aoi spent long periods in Japan, where he met other influential representatives of the design world, had several professional dealings with the Deska agency in Tokyo, and was invited to speak at Nawiwa University in Osaka and Musashino University in Tokyo. The Nippon Design Committee organised a one-man exhibition for him at the Matsuya design gallery, also in Tokyo.

top
Achille Castiglioni and Max
Huber
Record
study for watch dial, 1989
ø 30.2 mm (left) and
ø 36.14 mm

bottom
**Max Huber and
Achille Castiglioni with
the watch Record
manufactured by Alessi**
1989

Huber moved his work base to Nava Arti Grafiche in 1966, recalling the period when he had lived and worked at Einaudi immediately after the war. His nomadism, partly the product of a natural propensity for adaptation, again indicates the uninterrupted continuity between his life and profession. Throughout his life he shared studios with Massimo Vinelli, Waibl and Muratore, but never formed partnerships, preferring exchanges with other young designers. When he moved in permanently with Kono, his residences were always home-studios.

From 1968 to 1971, Huber worked on the design of the exhibition 'Magie des Papiers' (The Magic of Paper) at the Kunstgewerbemuseum Zürich (Zurich Museum of Decorative Arts), and he and Lanfranco Bombelli designed the graphics for the Expo 70 in Osaka from Barcelona. He continued working with Nava and producing graphic design work for exhibitions and initiatives in Zurich and Milan, winning first prize for his design for the 3rd International Biennale of Graphic Design in Brno with Castiglioni and exhibiting at the International Poster Biennale in Warsaw. He was frequently asked to sit on international juries, and he designed the communication for the Museum Bellerive and Kunstgewerbemuseum in Zurich.

In 1975, Michelangelo Antonioni asked him to create the titles for his documentary feature film *Chung-Kuo Cina* (Chung-Kuo China). He was a member of the Cantonal Commission for Fine Arts in Ticino and designed the image for several exhibitions at Palazzo Reale for the City of Milan including 'Burattini, Marionette, Pupi' (Puppeteers, Marionettes, Puppets) under Roberto Leydi.

From the early 1980s on, when the publisher Electa brought out the monograph *Max Huber: Progetti grafici 1936–1981* to Huber's own page design, he became increasingly involved in exhibitions of his own work, whether graphic design, photography or painting. He also created serigraphs at this time. He exhibited again in Brno, Warsaw, in Tokyo at 'Peace Poster', organized by the Japan Graphic Designers Association (1983), at the New York MoMA in the exhibition 'The Modern Poster' (1989), and in Toyama at several of the International Poster Triennials. He also designed the graphics for the dial of the Record watch designed by Achille Castiglioni for Alessi. He continued to work up until the very end of his life, when he died in Mendrisio, Switzerland, on 16 November 1992.

This never-ending list of connections, jobs and friendships helps explain how the quality of Huber's projects – and those of his contemporaries – was dependent upon exchanges between the various disciplines and branches of knowledge, a thick weave of relationships both personal and professional, and their remarkable skill for combining this variety of influences. Throughout his career, Huber worked with intellectual figures who saw the graphic designer's skill as a means to providing widespread visibility for many aspects of culture. He introduced a new compositional rigour to editorial projects such as periodicals (*Imballaggio* and *Sci*, and book series for ETAS, Einaudi, CIAM, etc.) and when he created advertisements for events and products, he used colour effects that were visual interpretations of rhythm (RAI TV, Borsalino hats, Braendli wallpaper, Niggeler & Küpfer textile group, Frisia mineral water, COIN department store); in interior designs (RAI TV, Milan Triennale, Mimusique, Sirenella Dancehall) he anticipated the archigraphics of recent years, and also, in his political and cultural engagements, he intuitively pre-empted digital experimentation (international contemporary music festivals, the music journal *Jazztime*, *Enciclopedia del Jazz* (Jazz Encyclopaedia), posters for the Premio Internazionale del film d'arte e sull'arte).

His projects constructed a clear sense of renewal through the coupling of new colour combinations with succinct texts. These were composed from letters that were hierarchically ordered into different groups – a large title, for example, with secondary information in much smaller type, gathered into

top left
Il terrorista (The Terrorist)
poster, 1962
370 x 260 mm

bottom left
Sala azzurra (Blue Room)
leaflet cover, 1977
310 x 220 mm

right
Burattini, marionette, pupi (Puppeteers, Marionettes, Puppets)
poster, 1980
230 x 235 mm

left
Sirenella Dancehall
poster, 1946
1400 x 1000 mm

right
Sirenella Dancehall
poster, 1946
700 x 1000 mm

sirenella

right
**Enciclopedia del Jazz
(Jazz Encyclopaedia)**
book cover, Edizioni
Messageria Musicali, 1952
245 x 180 mm

left
**New Orleans Roman Jazz
Band**
record cover, 1953–4
260 x 260 mm

'packages'. He also introduced strict grids that were easily identified due to text alignment. All this came about by virtue of a visual intelligence that favoured clarity, rhythm and synthesis. His projects, however, never lacked an experimental approach; he did not depart from a rigour that mediated closely between the impetus of the researcher and the client's needs. He would not hesitate to withdraw from a job in the face of requests he considered ludicrous, but was willing to review his plans if clients made useful suggestions.

At least three design types can be identified in Huber's work, which have been present throughout his career from the start. The first is typography combined with adjacent or overlapping colour backgrounds, examples of which can be found in the poster and programme for the 8th Milan Triennale in 1947 and in the series of studies for Coincidenze Arp and Art&Arp in 1991. Equally interesting are the projects produced by directly assembling the type while at the printer's, with no prior planning. Huber was sure of his ability to control the results, but curious as to possible unforeseen variables. The second category is analogical black and white pictures, illustrations or engravings, combined with a text and flat colour, as for the Einaudi book covers from the 1940s on, *Jazztime* in 1952 and the poster for the Chiasso Jazz Weeks in 1985. The third type of design identifiable in Huber's work concentrates on photographic experimentation and pure form combined with typography, as in the poster for the exhibition 'Abstrakt Konkret' in 1945 and the Niggeler & Küpfer monograph in 1976. The unframed black and white pictures, taken out of their context – often the same image repeated in different sizes – suggest a perception of the depth of field, while the flat backgrounds reiterate the two-dimensional nature of the paper; the same applies when the communication

right
Ritmo (Rythm)
magazine cover, Circolo
Amici del Jazz, 1950
310 x 210 mm

left
**Max Huber and Louis
Armstrong**
1949

used only typography. Nonetheless, superimposed texts in different sizes and colours suggest a sequence of possible levels, while still respecting the two-dimensional aspect. This is a distinctive feature of Huber's work: a sort of visual oxymoron in which the analogical reality of the photograph is 'extracted' from its context and linked with the undisguised printing techniques – flat colours, enlarged half-tone screen – upholding the choices through which his work is able to renew consolidated visual balances.

The time span covered by the list of examples above shows that the methods Huber adopted were never abandoned. His work was not subject to fashion or to substantial changes. The archetypes were always clear, from the beginning of his career to the end. His various strands of research ran in parallel, continuing the initial reference points acquired during the years of his training: typography, colour theory and exploring the potential of primary geometric forms. He employed the lesson learnt from Schawinsky and his experience with Studio Boggeri to develop his own personal vision of communication in which the use of colour was central to a clearer and more Italian vision. The constant presence of flat figures in his design, however, also links it to his original sources: the early avant-gardes, represented by Moholy Nagy, Piet Zwart, Bill and others.

In 'L'ideogramma cinestetico di Max Huber', dating from 1982, Giovanni Anceschi underlined the 'sonority' of Huber's design choices, especially in relation to the use of colour, following the experimental approach of the avant-gardes, who had often made attempts to highlight the affinities and links between colour and sound. This element of sound and the visual interpretation of rhythm and movement was close to Huber's heart. The archives contain a legacy of prizes, awards, texts, poetry, correspondence, but Huber's nature, his multi-faceted vision of the world and his capacity for visual synthesis are best summed up by the music he loved best: jazz. As Leydi recalls of the post-war years:

> Do you remember what Jazz meant to us, then? When we went to Malpensa [airport] in the lorry to collect Armstrong? Who does that any more? Armstrong was coming and we didn't work for a week. We just followed Armstrong. We weren't even kids. I was thirty. We were crazy. We could enjoy ourselves with nothing.[8]

One of the jobs that Huber executed with the greatest involvement and enthusiasm was the design of record covers, posters and publications for music events, jazz in particular. He designed posters and printed material for the Sirenella Dancehall, the cover of the journal *Ritmo* (Rythm), countless record covers for Parlophone, and the journal *Jazztime*, created with Leydi (few issues were published but it remains one of the most successful post-war music journals), he also used Armstrong's picture in the Braendli wallpaper 'Allegro ma non troppo'. He created the interior of the Arethusa Dancehall, decorating the ceiling with the soles of feet, which mirrored the dancing that would take place on the floor. He also designed sets for music events: a production of *Madame Butterfly* for television and *Mimusic no. 2 – Tre modi per sopportare la vita* (Three Ways to Bear Life), by Luciano Berio and Leydi for the Teatro delle Novità in Bergamo; he produced the graphics for the audience programmes and bills for the orchestra I Pomeriggi Musicali and the Festivals of Contemporary Music in Venice, at the request of Nando Ballo.

Like many young people of his generation, Huber loved jazz for the escape it offered in the post-war period, its potential for subversion, its charm, its free digression, its virtuosos and its repetitions. These were precisely the qualities that he saw in graphic design, which he used to redefine visual culture, thanks to a rare balance of control and innovation that has left its precious legacy to today's world.

Portfolio: Music

Max Huber designed many visual communication materials for activities with musical connections: magazines, posters, record covers, stage designs, interiors, among others. He saw music as a precise analogy of communication and faced the challenge of rendering rhythm visual with special enthusiasm. Above all, he loved jazz, perhaps because of its incomplete nature, the endless possible variations, the blend of harmonies and the obvious enjoyment of the performers, the need for rigorous execution and the unpredictable results, plus the sense of freedom it brought to a post-war Europe. The storage boxes for Huber's personal record collection, created from pictures cut out of newspapers, coloured paper collages, handwritten musicians' names, etc., and often featuring a circle or a spiral, are artworks in their own right, perfect hypothetical working models.

The series of covers for the magazine *Jazztime* has never been bettered and was produced with Roberto Leydi, a friend as well as a musical historian and critic, and a leading light, along with Luciano Berio, in the rebirth of music after the Second World War, especially in Milan. For every issue the masthead was repositioned beside silhouetted pictures of musicians, on which fragmented blocks of colour were superimposed (printing was in two colours in addition to black). The negative image – the white sheet – became the third colour, a left-over element contributing to the overall form. Nothing was left to chance; every component helped to construct the page, just as the sound and pauses of every instrument construct the sonority of music. The designs created for musical events rarely adopted direct analogical images, except for portraits of musicians: the music was represented through signs and colours, and the relationship between these elements provided an effective visual translation.

la biennale di venezia

teatro " la fenice „
5 - 19 settembre 1948

autunno musicale veneziano

XI. festival internazionale
di
musica contemporanea

XI Festival Internazionale
di Musica
Contemporanea (11th
Contemporary Music
International Festival)
programme cover, Venice
Biennale, 1948
245 x 170 mm

left
XI Festival Internazionale di Musica Contemporanea (11th Contemporary Music International Festival)
leaflet, Venice Biennale, 1948
173 × 200 mm

right
XII Festival Internazionale di Musica Contemporanea (12th Contemporary Music International Festival)
programme cover, Venice Biennale, 1949
245 × 345 mm

Max Huber

opposite and bottom
**Storage boxes for Max
Huber's jazz record
collection**
c. 1950
270 x 270 mm

opposite and bottom
Storage boxes for Max Huber's jazz record collection
c. 1950
270 x 270 mm

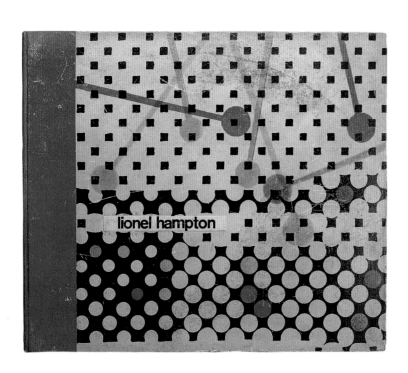

jazztime

and records

jazztime
and records

vuole essere
una rivista sinceramente moderna
viva e polemica

dedicata in serietà e attenzione
alla vita e ai problemi
di tutto il jazz
di ieri, di oggi e di domani

perciò la sua bandiera non è
nè quella del bop
nè quella del dixieland

piuttosto quella ben più gloriosa
della musica
senza aggettivi

amministrazione e pubblicità
via L. Cagnola, 8
Milano

Prezzo L. 300

opposite and right
**Voci e immagini del 1958
(Voices and images of
1958)**
record covers, 1958
310 x 310 mm

IX Autunno Musicale (9th
Musical Autumn Festival)
poster, Como, 1975
1000 x 700 mm

Portfolio: La Rinascente

Max Huber's first major design project was for the department store La Rinascente. He had already worked on other corporate identity projects, but here the sheer number and different types of products, plus the rapid turnover of advertising, forced him to adopt a new design pace, a foretaste of what would soon become common practice in advertising agencies.

The store was investing in visual communication and, above all, seeking to establish what has more recently been called a 'corporate image'. This meant proposing a new lifestyle, a medium-high consumerist model – tennis, golf, skiing, home furnishings – that exploited the imagery of film. La Rinascente was able to promote its products so successfully thanks to the presence of Albe Steiner as art director of the Advertising Office from 1950 to 1954. He and Carlo Pagani, the in-house communication co-ordinator, promoted the 'Compasso d'Oro – per l'estetica del prodotto' (The Golden Compass – For Beautiful Products), an award and exhibition that focused attention on the aesthetic properties of everyday objects and the increasingly crucial role being played by designers and manufacturing firms.

Huber was required to renew the store's visual communication strategy, avoiding repetition while reiterating its existing identity through every commodity and each advertising campaign. He managed to do this by adopting a method that was ahead of its time. Instead of systematically repeating the structure of one advertisement, he used his own language and his own archetypes to represent the store's activities and initiatives. He always employed visual texture to represent the company, suggesting the fabric behind the La Rinascente reality. From the wrapping paper to the advertisements, the spiral logo, designed in 1950, was always present, as were the silhouetted images of glasses, gloves, skiers, cyclists and models, superimposed on flat backgrounds in special colours that reduced the subject to pure form and constructed the rhythm of the page.

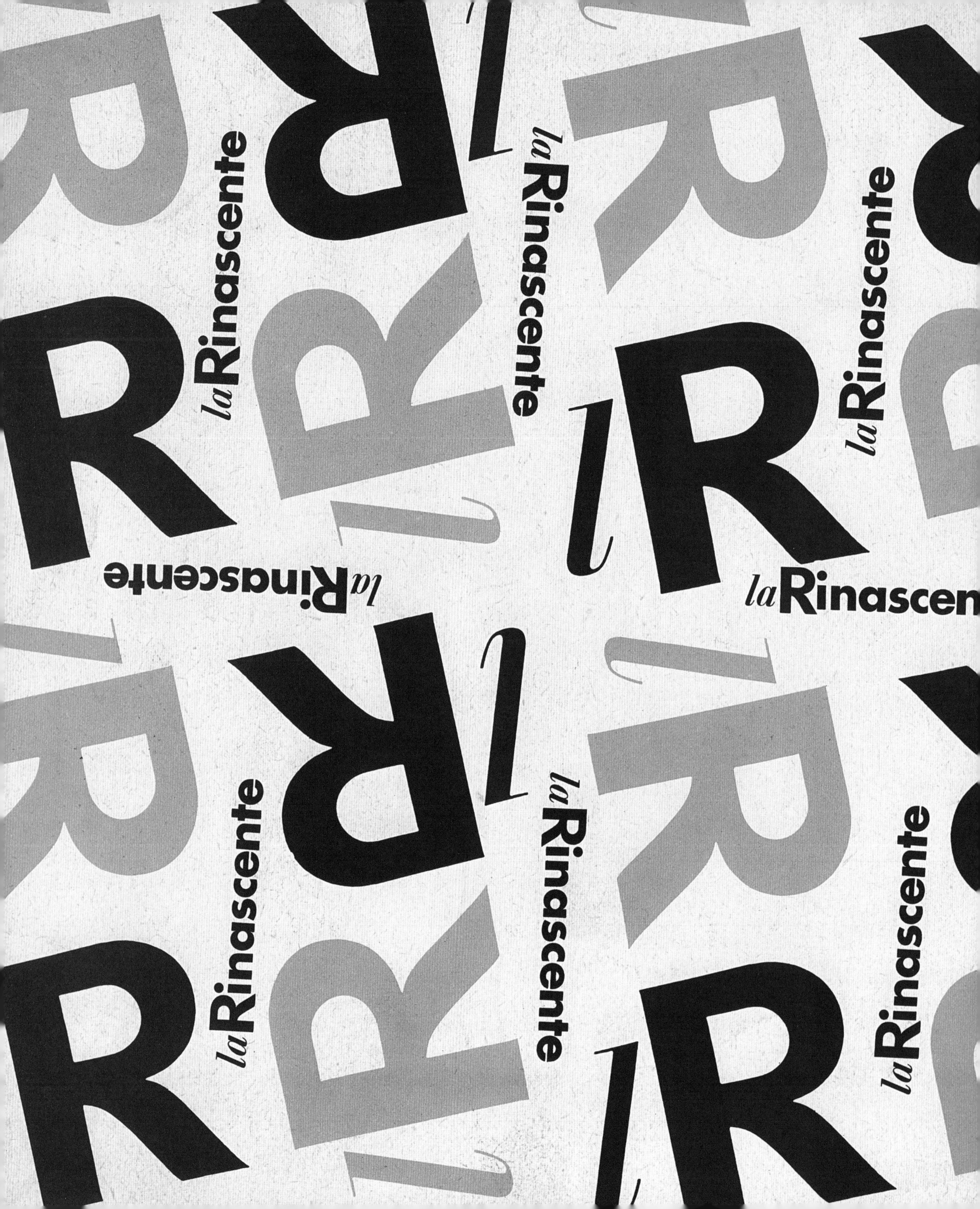
laRinascente

opposite
La Rinascente
wrapping paper, 1950

top left
La Rinascente: Moda maschile (Men's Fashion)
wrapping paper, 1953

top right
La Rinascente: L'estate consiglia (Summer Fashion)
wrapping paper, 1953

bottom left and right
La Rinascente: Auguri (Season's Greetings)
wrapping paper, 1951

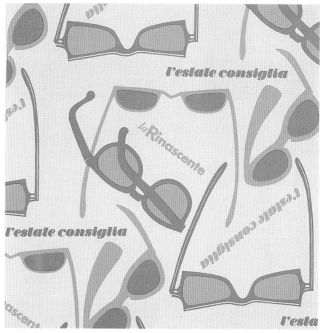

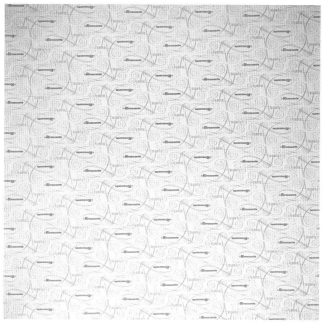

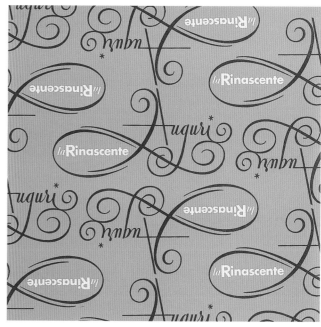

top left, top right and
bottom left
La Rinascente
advertisements, 1951
290 x 150 mm

bottom right
**La Rinascente: Apertura
di stagione (New Season)**
brochure cover, 1951
170 x 120 mm

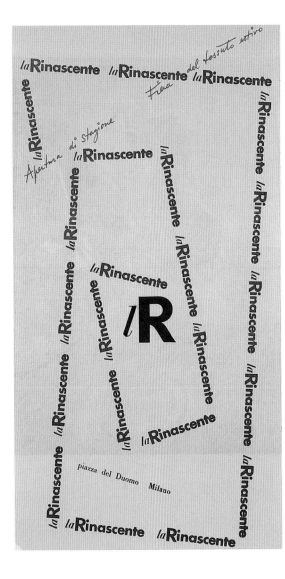

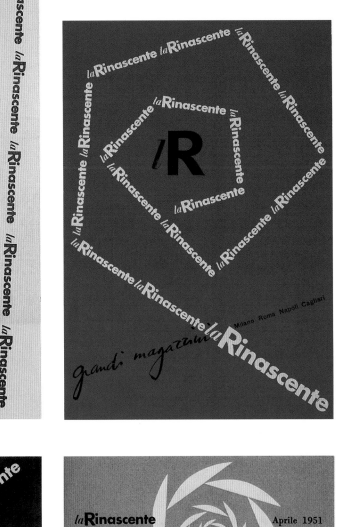

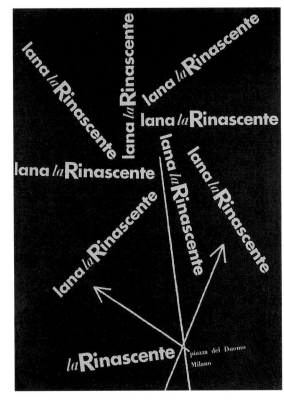

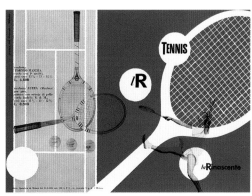

cente - Upim

ica mattina 6 luglio

i per 500.000 lire

Km 165

. Pi... Trezzo d'Adda Vimercate Monza Milano

e-Upim Milano via Giovenale 15 telefono 31102

n data 20-6-1952

I. G. D. A. - Novara 1952

Coppa La Rinascente-
Upim (La Rinascente-
UPIM Bicycle Race)
poster, 1952
700 x 1000 mm

la**R**inascente *calze*

Una visita al nostro reparto Calze
vi permetterà di scegliere
nel vastissimo nostro assortimento,
di produzione nazionale ed estera,
dove l'eccellenza del prodotto si unisce
all'equità del prezzo.

*l*R

CALZE *8-20 gennaio*

la**R**inascente

Max Huber

opposite top
**La Rinascente: Calze
(Sockings)**
brochure cover, 1952
250 x 190 mm

opposite bottom
**La Rinascente: L'inverno
consiglia (Winter Season)**
catalogue covers, 1952–3
310 x 235 mm

top left
**La Rinascente: Harry
Rosenfeld**
leaflet, 1953
150 x 300 mm

top right
La Rinascente: Elle Erre
advertisement, 1952
290 x 110 mm

bottom
**La Rinascente: Ho la mia
casa (My Own House)**
brochure cover, 1954
215 x 240 mm

left
La Rinascente
leaflet, 1953
140 x 140 mm

top right and centre right
**La Rinascente: Primavera
1953 (Spring 1953)**
brochure (verso and recto),
1953
205 x 285 mm

bottom right
**La Rinascente: Apertura
di stagione (New Season)**
leaflet, 1953
350 x 350 mm

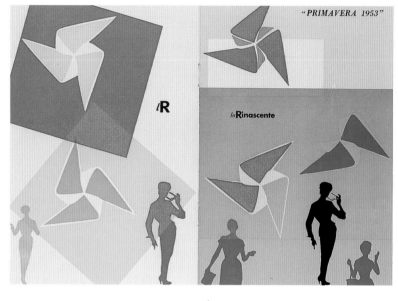

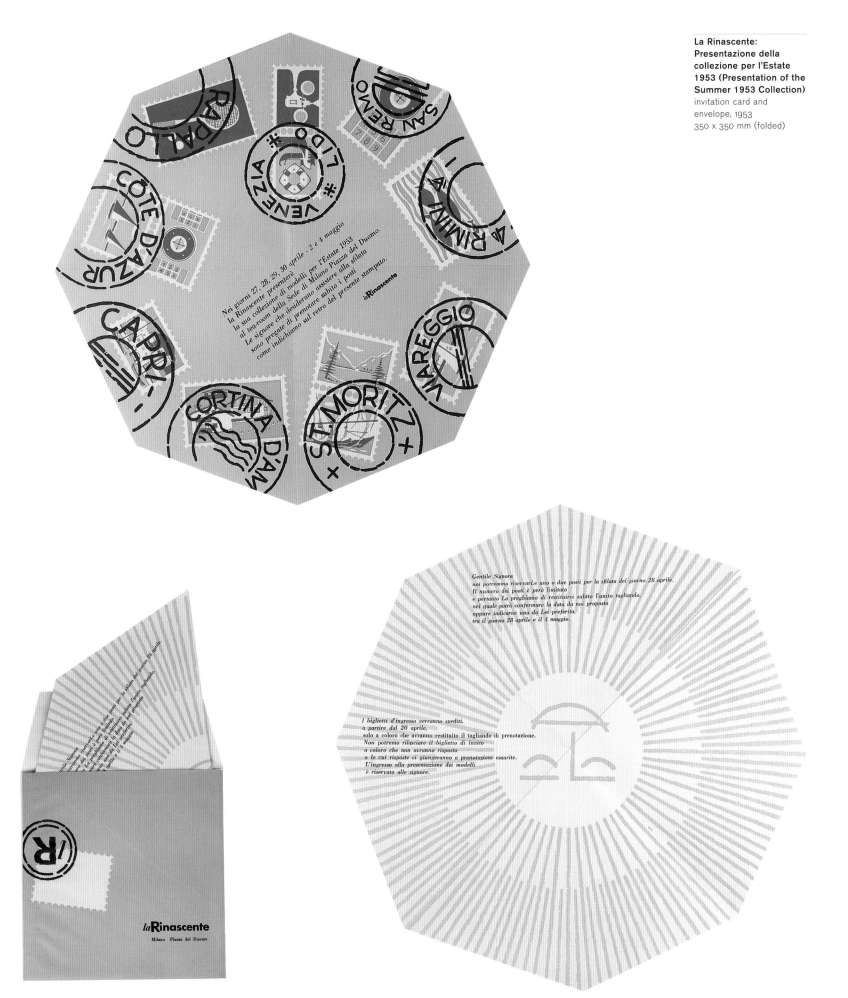

**La Rinascente:
Presentazione della
collezione per l'Estate
1953 (Presentation of the
Summer 1953 Collection)**
invitation card and
envelope, 1953
350 x 350 mm (folded)

Nei giorni 27, 28, 29, 30 aprile · 2 e 4 maggio
la Rinascente presenterà
la sua collezione di modelli per l'Estate 1953
al tea-room della Sede di Milano Piazza del Duomo.
Le signore che desiderano assistere alla sfilata
sono pregate di prenotare subito i posti
come indichiamo sul retro del presente stampato.

Gentile Signora
noi potremmo riservarLe uno o due posti per la sfilata del giorno 28 aprile.
Il numero dei posti è però limitato
e pertanto La preghiamo di restituirci subito l'unito tagliando,
nel quale potrà confermare la data da noi proposta
oppure indicarne una da Lei preferita,
tra il giorno 28 aprile e il 4 maggio.

I biglietti d'ingresso verranno spediti,
a partire dal 20 aprile,
solo a coloro che avranno restituito il tagliando di prenotazione.
Non potremo rilasciare il biglietto di invito
a coloro che non avranno risposto
o le cui risposte ci giungeranno a prenotazioni esaurite.
L'ingresso alla presentazione dei modelli
è riservato alle signore.

la Rinascente
Milano Piazza del Duomo

top
**La Rinascente: Moda
autunno inverno 1955
(Autumn Winter 1955)**
poster, 1955
700 x 1000 mm

bottom left
**La Rinascente: Per lo
stile d'inverno (Winter
Style)**
catalogue cover, 1955
290 x 240 mm

bottom right
**La Rinascente: L'estate
1955 consiglia (Summer
1955)**
catalogue cover, 1955
290 x 240 mm

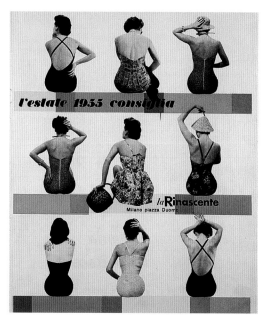

Affiss. Autorizz. in tutta Italia dalla Questura di Milano in data 26-2-55   Cartotecnica RIBOLDI-Milano

facciamo primavera insieme

Stampa propagandistica tassa pagata
autorizz. N 1535 del 23-2-1955 della
Direzione Provinciale delle Poste e
Telegrafi di Milano

la**Rinascente**

top
**La Rinascente: La moda
di primavera (Spring
Fashion)**
poster, 1955
700 x 1000 mm

bottom
**La Rinascente: Facciamo
primavera insieme (Let's
Make Spring Together)**
envelope, 1955
85 x 250 mm

top
La Rinascente: Casalinghi arredamento (Interior Design for the Home)
poster, 1958
70 x 100 mm

bottom
La Rinascente: Il Giappone (Japan)
brochure, 1956
230 x 230 mm

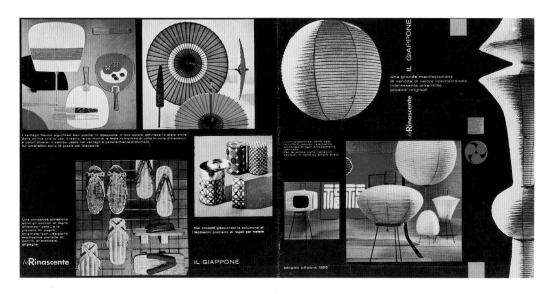

Portfolio: Mass Media

Immediately after the First World War, radio was the primary source of advertising directed at Italian families; radio broadcasts from the 1930s on availed themselves of private sponsorship, following the US example. In 1934, for instance, 'I Quattro Moschettieri' (The Four Musketeers) was sponsored by Perugina, the confectionery manufacturer and was combined with a highly successful competition. However, it was not until after the Second World War that radio took on a truly significant role as an essential means of communicating information, although without sacrificing its commercial side.

Italy's first TV broadcasts, from RAI headquarters in Turin, began on just one channel on 3 January 1954. In Europe – England, France, Germany and Italy – radio and television originated as public broadcasting systems bound to the state, unlike the US model. In Italy, public financing – partly through the payment of a licence fee – meant that large sums of money could be allocated to communicating the service's existence, and for the permanent acquisition of exhibition space in the Fiera Campionaria (Milan Trade Fair) in Milan.

The quality of the communication was strictly controlled by RAI and the advertising projects and exhibition designs were assigned to the best designers available: the radio and TV opening tunes were created by Erberto Carboni, much of the printed material by Max Huber, Remo Muratore and Albe Steiner, and the exhibition designs by the Castiglioni brothers, with Huber's assistance for the architectural graphics, and subsequently by Enzo Mari.

left
Il Giornale Radio (Radio News)
book cover, 1948
115 x 175 mm

right
BBC: English by Radio no. 2
booklet cover, 1948
215 x 140 mm

opposite
I Esposizione Internazionale di Televisione (1st International Television Exhibition)
brochure cover, Palazzo dell'Arte, Milan, 1949
200 x 210 mm

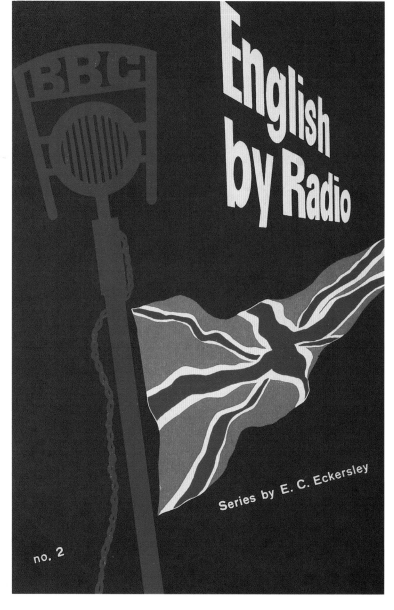

televisione

Palazzo dell'Arte al Parco di Milano
10 - 19 Settembre 1949

1ª esposizione internazionale di televisione

La ripresa di una scena televisiva avviene, all'incirca, con un procedimento analogo a quello adoperato in cinematografia. Al posto della comune macchina da ripresa usata per il cinema, si adopera una speciale camera da presa che contiene un particolare tipo di valvola elettronica. Valvola che opera la trasformazione delle varie immagini in una serie di impulsi elettrici, i quali vengono trasmessi con un ponte-radio alla stazione trasmittente che li amplifica e li trasmette al ricevitore televisivo. Questi, a sua volta, ricostituisce l'immagine trasmessa e la proietta sullo schermo dell'apparecchio.

Alfieri & Lacroix - Milano   max huber

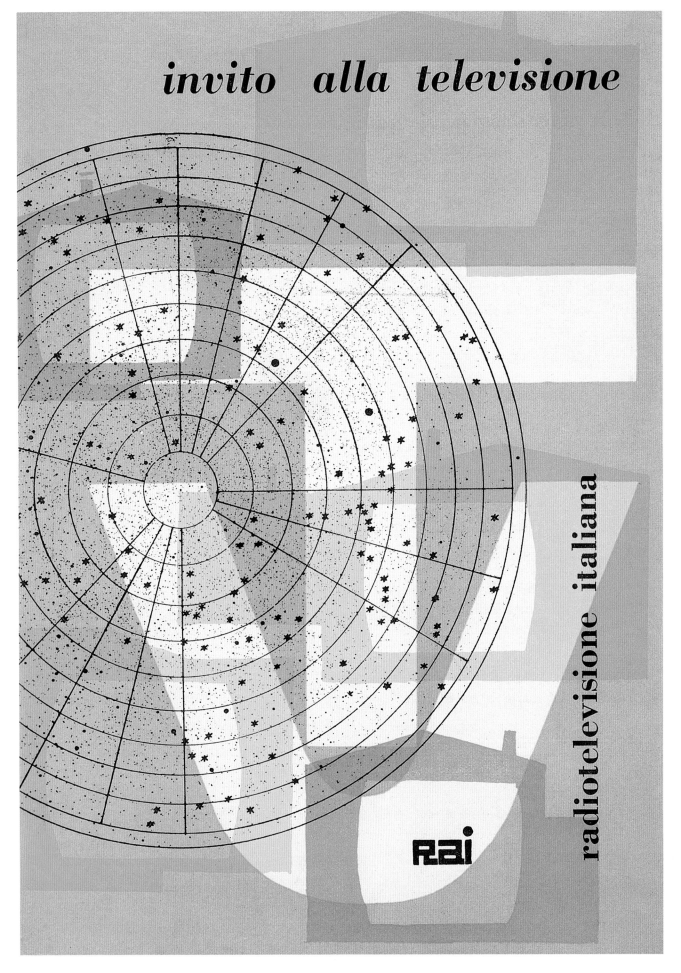

invito alla televisione

radiotelevisione italiana

rai

left
**RAI: invito alla televisione
(RAI: Invitation to
Television Viewing)**
booklet cover, c. 1955
210 x 150 mm

opposite top
**Radio Televisione
Elettroacustica 1959–60
(Electroacoustic Radio
and Television 1959–60)**
catalogue cover, 1959
325 x 210 mm

opposite bottom
**Mostra Nazionale della
Radio e Televisione
(National Radio and
Television Exhibition)**
award certificate, 1959
240 x 380 mm

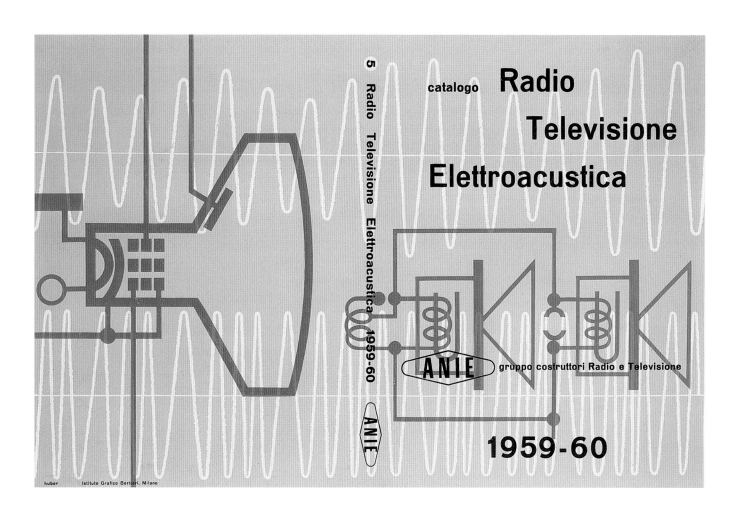

la Mostra Nazionale della Radio e Televisione
per solennizzare
la sua venticinquesima edizione conferisce
la medaglia di bronzo a

_____

per aver partecipato
dal 1947 al 1959 a dieci manifestazioni.

_____

il segretario

_____

il presidente del comitato organizzatore
capo gruppo XV° RTV · ANIE

Milano, 12 - 21 Settembre 1959

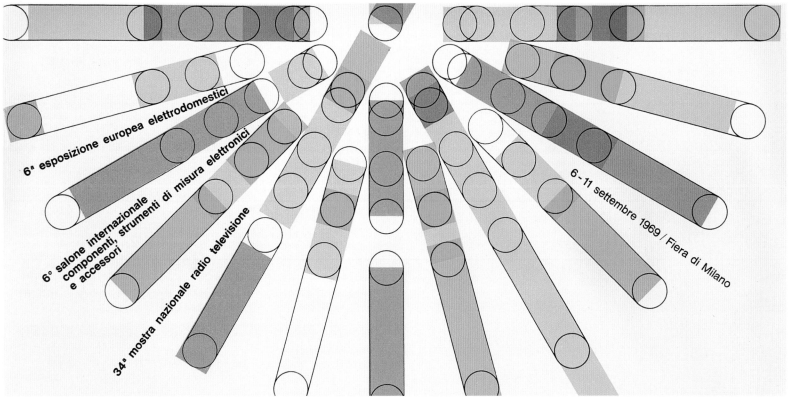

ANIE
gruppo costruttori radio e televisione

Radio Televisione
Elettroacustica

catalogo

1967-68

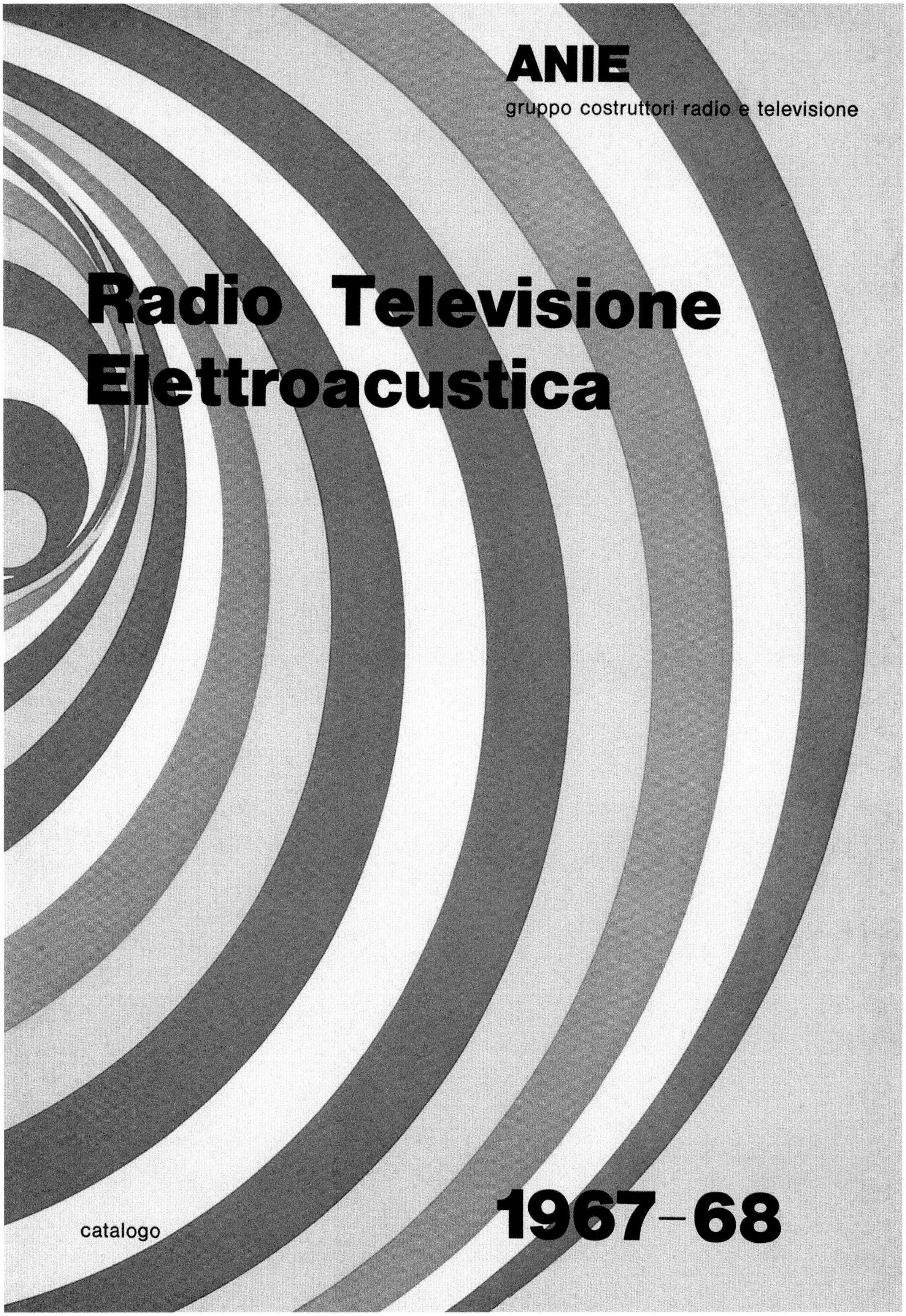

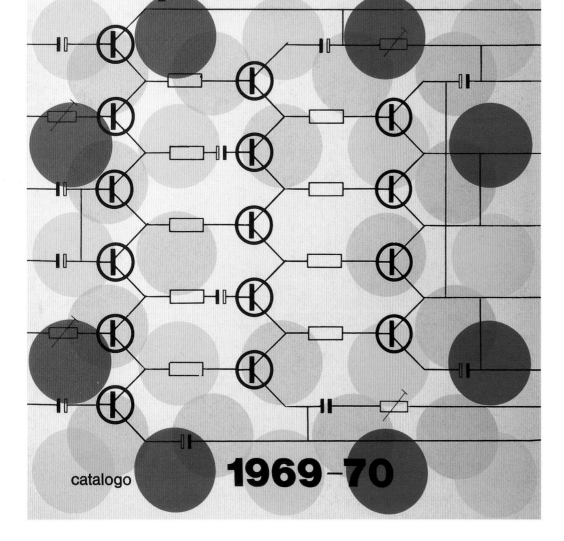

ANIE
gruppo costruttori radio e televisione
gruppo componenti elettronici

Radio Televisione
Elettroacustica
Componenti elettronici

catalogo 1969-70

Radio Televisione
Elettroacustica
Componenti elettronici
1969–70 (Electroacoustic
Radio and Television:
Electronic Parts)
catalogue cover, 1969
205 x 145 mm

Portfolio: Publishing

Italy's cultural isolation during the twenty-year Fascist period, prompted by the regime's desire to maximise nationalistic traditions, generated a desire for exchanges with different cultures and points of view after the Second World War. Interest focused on the United States for its music, literature and advertising and on the Eastern European countries, the USSR in particular, since (in intent at least), they represented a more equal vision of society.

The publishing industry – daily newspapers and periodicals included – experienced a remarkable boom; the first illustrated weeklies and monthlies had unexpectedly large circulation numbers for a country in which there was still a high percentage of illiteracy. Many of the new publishers (including Einaudi and Feltrinelli) were Left-leaning politically, and thanks to Elio Vittorini, Italo Calvino, Cesare Pavese and Beppe Fenoglio, Einaudi promoted the new American writers. These young editors, writers themselves, turned to the professionalism of young graphic artists with similar experiences and culture. In 1945, Albe Steiner designed *Il Politecnico* for Giulio Einaudi and Max Huber worked on the book series Biblioteca del Politecnico (Polytechnic Library) which openly evoked the rigid graphics of the post-First World War Soviet and German avant gardes. Huber's most interesting works, however, were those for Einaudi and Etas Kompass, in which attention was focused on lettering and a careful and elegant use of colour, which as time progressed became desaturated: the use of primary colours and the combination of red and black became rarer. Black and white photography was overlayed with flat colour backgrounds that took it beyond descriptive realism. Systematic collaboration with publishers allowed Huber to create entire series over which he had ongoing project control, not just in terms of the initial approach but also over the design of every single cover.

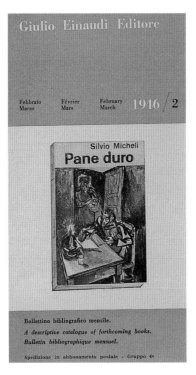

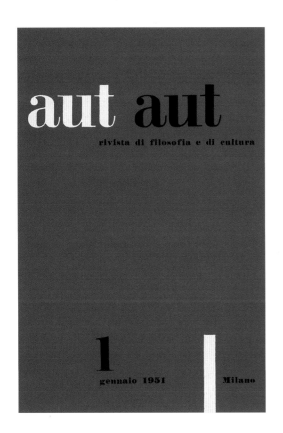

Gabriele Morello

e petrolio
e sud
inchiesta a Ragusa

ETAS editrice

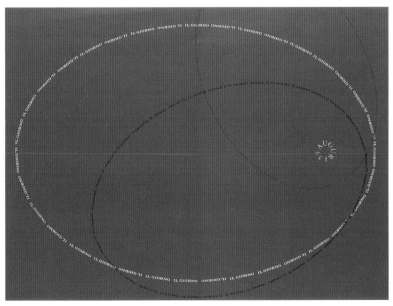

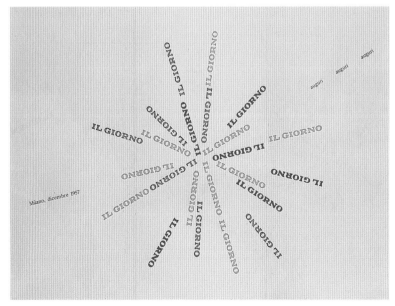

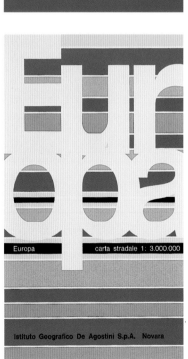

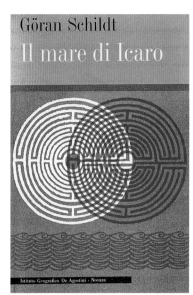

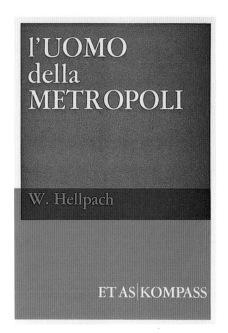

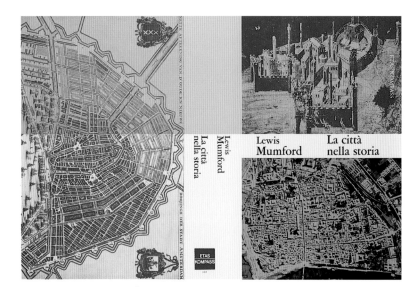

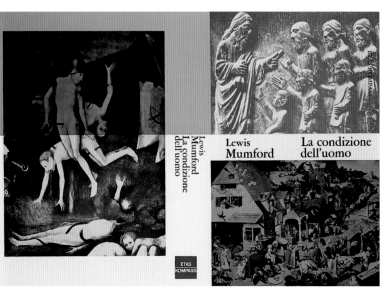

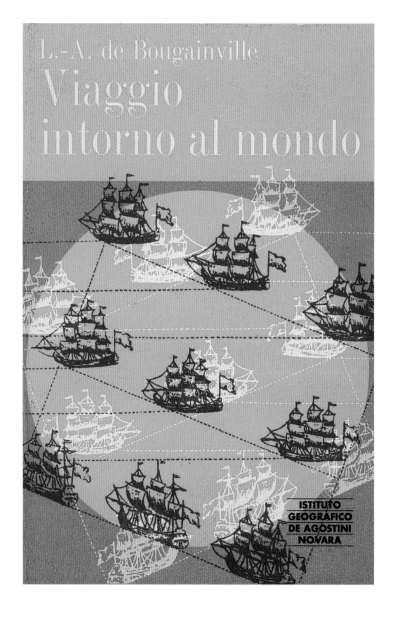

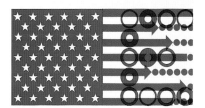

Jean-Jacques Servan-Schreiber
La sfida americana
prefazione di Ugo La Malfa

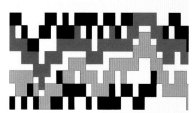

Francesco Forte
La strategia delle riforme

Adolf A. Berle
La repubblica economica americana

nuova collana di saggi 1

ETAS KOMPASS

nuova collana di saggi 4

ETAS KOMPASS

nuova collana di saggi 5

ETAS KOMPASS

Kenneth E. Boulding
Il significato del XX secolo
Verso una società post-civile

nuova collana di saggi 19

ETAS KOMPASS

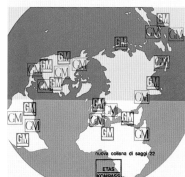

Frederic G. Donner
L'impresa multinazionale
L'espansione mondiale della General Motors

nuova collana di saggi 22

ETAS KOMPASS

La Cina dopo la rivoluzione culturale
a cura di
Dick Wilson

saggi di
Adie / Gittings / Wylie
Dernberger / Gray
Fitzgerald / Harris
Lindbeck / Yahuda
Selk / Oldham

nuova collana di saggi 25

ETAS KOMPASS

Max Huber: Archigraphic Designer
Giampiero Bosoni

Max Huber at the RAI
Pavilion
1948

3

Max Huber: Archigraphic Designer

Having been personally acquainted with Max Huber, I do not find it easy to adopt the detached stance of the historian and look at his work with a scholarly, scientific eye. Huber was what in Italy we call 'a force of nature'. He was a splendid mix: he had irrepressible natural talent and a faultless drawing hand; he possessed the lively candour of the eternal child; he was a true product of the rigorous Swiss school; he loved innovatory research; he boasted a lively curiosity, being quick to latch on – not without irony – to the most unpredictable ideas; and he worked with the serious precision of the first-rate professional. Not only was he the outstanding graphic designer we all know, but he was also a good artist and, above all, a gifted archigraphic designer (in the sense of graphics with a three-dimensional function and true spatial value), particularly in the fields of temporary architecture and industrial design.

Discovering Exhibition Design, 1935–40

Huber's interest in architecture – modern architecture in particular (in the form of light structures made from modular units) – was demonstrated in the early years of his training by a photographic report that he produced on his visit to the 'Schweizerische Landesausstellung' (Swiss National Fair) in Zurich in 1939, which was clearly inspired by Constructivist and Bauhaus shooting techniques.[1] This encounter with the world of major exhibition communication was a great stimulus for Huber: 'There were wonderful things there … one was Heinrich Steiner's graphic work for the Sport pavilion. Fantastic! Then, there was a tower for the pharmaceutical industry … I still have some photographs I took of that event.'[2] It is interesting to note that none of those surviving photographs are of the graphic work mentioned – Steiner's sketches for the Sport pavilion, for example, or those by his friends Werner Bishof, for the pavilion 'Paper, Graphic Design, Surveying, Film, Photography', and Max Bill, for the Bauen pavilion. What do remain are research photographs taken at angles that markedly suggest the influence of the New Objectivity, interpretations of the bold, modern proposals for the structural, communicational and playful dimension of the exhibition space.

The treatment of exhibition space as a research tool, design model, prototype or manifesto of new creative trends was a constant presence in the training of the twentieth-century architectural and artistic avant-gardes. They saw this space – timeless and weightless, in a certain sense, given its less portentous architectural status – as an ideal void in which to achieve the purest expression of uncontaminated design. This was not always painstaking but often instinctive and unpredictable like certain exhibition designs in which the same ideal was symbolically represented. 'Think of the pavilions created by Le Corbusier, El Lissitzky', Huber often said.[3]

In 1935, at the age of sixteen, Huber enrolled at the Kunstgewerbeschule Zürich (Zurich School of Arts and Crafts), where Ernst Gubler, Gottlieb Wehrli,

opposite
**Schweizerische
Landesausstellung (Swiss
National Fair)**
view of the entrance to the
Sport Pavilion, 1939

top
**Schweizerische
Landesausstellung (Swiss
National Fair)**
interior view of the
Aluminium Pavilion, 1939

bottom
**Schweizerische
Landesausstellung (Swiss
National Fair)**
view of the Chemistry
Pavilion, 1939

Heiri Müller, Walter Roshardt, Otto Weber and Alfred Willimann were teachers. The latter, in particular, with his exciting lessons on the history of art and graphics, became the young Huber's point of reference. Willimann suggested that Huber should spend time in the school library, where he discovered the experiments of the Bauhaus, the formulae and solutions of Jan Tschichold's New Printing, as well as European abstract art. It is highly likely that, among other things, Huber also read about the exhibition techniques studied at the Bauhaus by the graphic designer Herbert Bayer, the 'screaming' propaganda pavilions of the Russian Constructivists and contemporary Swiss work. He probably encountered the 1924–5 Co-Op windows in Ghent and Basel by Hannes Meyer, the Swiss pavilion designed by Hans Hofmann for the Pressa Fair in Cologne in 1928 (featuring a famous exhibition design by El Lissitzky for the USSR section), H Fischer's studies for a modular travelling stand in 1936, and Bill's important design of the Swiss section of the 6th Milan Triennale in 1936.[4] This last discovery may have fuelled Huber's desire to meet Bill and probably later influenced his decision to gain work experience in Milan.

It is not easy to pinpoint Huber's first exhibition design. Unfortunately the archive records for that period seem to be incomplete. This uncertainty is endorsed by certain biographies (edited by Huber himself) that state, for instance, that 'he spent entire evenings painting texts on panels in three languages with Miedinger and Schulthess',[5] who designed the national exhibition in 1939. No other evidence remains of his involvement in the Zurich exhibition, but it would appear that it was restricted to manual labour, with Huber making no contribution to the design itself.

Milan and Studio Boggeri, 1940–1

In order to find more substantial records of his early exhibition work, we must move on to Huber's first experience in Milan with Studio Boggeri, in 1940 and 1941. The Studio Boggeri environment was especially stimulating for the young Huber; although he still could not speak a word of Italian, his open mind and Boggeri's warm welcome quickly brought him into contact with numerous graphic artists, photographers, artists and architects on the dynamic Milanese scene, with whom he exchanged ideas, made friends and embarked on professional ventures. During this period he also visited the exhibitions held at Palazzo dell'Arte, including the 7th Milan Triennale of 1940, where he was greatly impressed by some of the exhibition designs. He particularly admired that of the small room devoted to the master plan for the Isle of Elba designed by BBPR (Gian Luigi Banfi, Lodovico Barbiano di Belgiojoso, Enrico Peressutti and Ernesto Nathan Rogers) and was even more taken by that for the 'International Exhibition of Mass Production', curated by Giuseppe Pagano with the assistance of a large work team.[6] In this latter design, Huber was struck by the lightness of the exhibition system, which had been created through the use of interlaced metal cables. Several elements were suspended from the complex, including one that could not but catch the eye of the Concrete artist – an aerial communication sculpture-structure, hanging in the centre of the hall. Some passages on the contents of this exhibition, published in the 7th Milan Triennale catalogue, suggest what might have triggered Huber's interest in this part of the exhibition. The core theme of this section was 'standards', understood in the exhibition as 'humankind's search for absolute laws governing rhythm and aesthetic relations and the tendency to create effective organisms for the study and regulation of type standardization … these principles do not represent a cold mechanization of life, they are part of the natural economy of organized life, for the most part made up of combinations of concepts or mass-produced objects.'[7]

top
Max Huber for Studio
Boggeri
Olivetti: Studio 42
window display design, 1943

bottom
**Stampa Socialista
(Socialist Press)**
exhibition design, Zurich,
1944

opposite top
Sirenella Dancehall
mural, Milan, 1949

bottom
**Il socialismo vivrà!
(Socialism Lives On!)**
exhibition design, Milan,
1945

To return to Huber's involvement in the design of exhibition spaces, his archives contain two photographs of a design for an Olivetti shop, which can confidently be dated between the late 1930s and the mid-1940s, since the subject of the display is the Studio 42 typewriter designed by Luigi Figini and Gino Pollini with Xanti Schawinsky. This went into production in 1935 and was replaced in 1950 by the Lettera 22, designed by Marcello Nizzoli. According to several letters conserved in the Boggeri Archive,[8] Huber continued to collaborate with Studio Boggeri from Switzerland through correspondence, but no records prove that he was responsible for this Olivetti project. Nonetheless, the project clearly shows the typical Boggeri approach, with the subtle shop sign that plays on a shift in perception through its use of disproportionate elements. For example, a large magnified lever in the background is combined with abstract lattices (close to Huber's figurative language) representing the microcrystalline compounds of the various steels used in the mechanical parts of the typewriters. However, it is more likely that this project was the work of Giovanni Pintori, Olivetti's in-house graphic artist, because some of the advertising pages[9] he designed to promote the Studio 42 typewriter contain the same microcrystalline graphics, as well as axonometric drawings closely resembling the pieces suspended in the shop design. Huber's style is more easily identified in a picture that can be found in the book *Max Huber: progetti grafici 1936–1981*,[10] edited by Huber himself; this shows another design detail for an Olivetti shop window, dated 1943, in which we see hexagonal spirals and photographic effects typical of his work. This publication may confirm his ongoing long-distance collaboration with Studio Boggeri. It would certainly explain why Huber's archives contain photographs of the design probably created by Pintori, as reference material supplied by Olivetti for the study of the new design to promote the Studio 42 typewriter.

Early Experiences in Switzerland, 1941–5

During the war years, Huber worked as a graphic artist for the journal *Du* in Switzerland, as well as focusing on the artistic research that would, in 1942, lead him to join Allianz Vereiningung moderner Schweizer Künstler (Alliance, the Association of Modern Swiss Artists), a group of modern Swiss artists led by Max Bill. On the subject of graphic projects carried into three-dimensional space, Huber's biographies[11] tell of two jobs with Bishof – the designs for the exhibition 'The Colour of Photography' at the Kunstgewerbemuseum and for the Stoffel pavilion at the Zurich Fashion Week. Again, regrettably, no trace of these projects exists in the Huber archives. What does surface from these years is work for the *Stampa socialista* (Socialist Press) that can be dated to 1944. The designer is not named but Huber's contribution is clearly evident in the communication panels and glass cases, based on the principles conceptualized by Bayer at the Bauhaus, and in the construction of a virtual wall structure with a close-packed row of wooden bars arranged vertically to serve as a layout grid.

Commitment and Verve in the Reconstruction of Milan, 1945–8

Huber's return to Milan in October 1945 marked the beginning of his real experience in the field of exhibition design. The social context, with which he quickly caught up, was no longer constrained and suffocated by the Fascist regime. It was a new and exciting time in the country's civil reconstruction, emerging as it was from serious defeat with a strong, sure spirit of democratic and cultural rebirth. Everything was moving on with great enthusiasm and verve and this greatly stimulated the young graphic artist from the north. Within the space of a few months, the free and exuberant circulation of ideas led to encounters with many of the leading intellectuals, writers, artists, architects and publishers active in Milan and Turin, all passionately engaged in this liberating cultural rebirth of the nation.

It is interesting to note that Huber's first experiences in three-dimensional space during this period were produced with considerable impetus, almost faster than the printed works. They consisted of two decorative-pictorial projects, both produced in 1946: murals for the Sirenella dancehall in Milan and for Braendli, a wallpaper manufacturer, which had a display at the first RIMA (Riunione Italiana Mostre Arredamento – Italian Interior Design Exhibitions)[12] exhibition at Palazzo dell'Arte (the traditional venue of the Milan Triennale exhibitions), again in the provincial capital. These projects combine Huber's two passions in an attempt to vitalize the space: visual art and jazz. Rhythmic, dynamic geometries, kaleidoscopic reflections, fireworks, drum rolls and jazz trumpet phrases were the motifs he used for the swinging dance venue planned for young people, as well as for his appealing backdrop for the small commercial display corner.

In the same year, Huber helped create two exhibition designs focusing on the political theme of the Resistance, to which he was ideologically close. The first was designed with Remo Muratore. The other, entitled 'Il socialismo vivrà!' (Socialism Lives On!) was in collaboration with Paolo Grassi (one of the founders of the theatre Piccolo Teatro in Milan) and was backed by the Socialist newspaper *Avanti*. Regrettably, there is no trace of the first project in the Huber archives but some surviving pictures of the second suggest that he was responsible for the entire exhibition-design project. The extreme simplicity of the project, in part due to obvious financial restraints, involved graphic panels created by applying photographs and original documents (mainly newspapers and journals) to backgrounds pre-designed with strong graphic signs (arrows, wedge shapes, triangles and squares). It is likely that each of the panels made major use of the colour red and can therefore be clearly understood as a Constructivist exercise, much inspired by El Lissitzky. The strong point of the exhibition was, however, a small, lightweight display structure, which received decidedly more attention than the panels. Hooked to a trellis at the front, which was made of three crossed sticks, were several small communicational elements. A panel, raised above the floor and completely covered with newspaper pages, served as a background and developed a concave relationship to the trellis through its curvilinear profiles at top and bottom. Suspended from it was a large disc bearing the phrase 'Il socialismo vivrà!' in huge letters. This display sums up Huber's passion for the propaganda message typical of the Russian avant-garde, but he introduces a fresh and original personal approach through the curved, plastic and dynamic forms and the shifting spatial perception.

Between 1946 and 1947, Huber began work on two major projects that would propel him into the world of modern architectural and artistic research in the reborn Milan. These were the design of the coordinated graphics for the 8th Milan Triennale of 1947 with Albe Steiner, and his almost simultaneous collaboration with Lanfranco Bombelli and Bill on the exhibition 'Arte astratta e concreta' (Abstract and Concrete Art) to be held at Palazzo Reale in Milan.

'There was a great deal of enthusiasm for the 8th Triennale, that of 1947, when I started assisting with it', commented Huber, 'because it was the first Triennale after Fascism'.[13] The graphic design was first entrusted to Steiner, who created the T8 logo and started work on the coordinated image. But when he found he had to go on a long trip to Mexico, he asked his friend and colleague, whose design concepts were close to his own, to take over and develop the work he had already set up. Huber adhered to Steiner's choices but expanded on them with some of his own ideas. Reference to the exhibition catalogue[14] reveals Huber's hand in various spheres. He is credited five times on pages 14 and 15 of the general exhibition organization plan, presumably in each case for the graphic design. These credits include his work on the T8 catalogue-guide with architects L Bombelli and E Gentili;

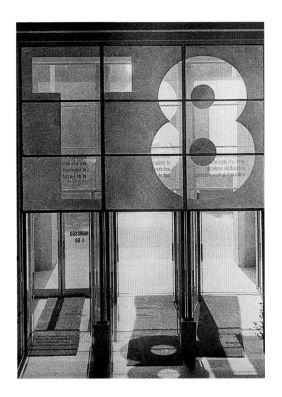

the entire general exhibition design with architects A Bianchetti, V Magistretti and M Tedeschi; the 'Mostra Internazionale Fotografica dell'Architettura' (International Architectural Photography Exhibition) with Bombelli and Gentili (p. 39); the furnishings sector with the architects L Canella, A Castelli Ferrieri, Ghidini and Ravasi (p. 122) and the exhibition 'Propaganda' with the architects Bombelli, E Bonini and Steiner. Further on, we also find that Huber sat on the jury of the second Italviscosa competition for upholstery designs and won first prize in the competition for Braendli wallpaper designs. Moreover, on page 19, we read that the architect Tedeschi, in collaboration with Huber, won the 'competition for an advertising structure to be placed on the flowerbed facing the Nord-Milano station in Piazzale Cadorna during T8'. This advertising stand was never built, although another structure in tubular metal was constructed for the announcement of the 'Competition to Win a Home'; designed by Bianchetti and Pea, it was installed both in the centre of Galleria Vittorio Emanuele[15] and in Piazza del Duomo. This project does not appear among those listed in the catalogue but the fact that pictures of this ultra-lightweight stand, with an obviously Constructivist composition that includes megaphones, are in the Huber archives would suggest that he was responsible for the graphics on the panels hanging in the centre of the structure, and perhaps had a hand in the abstract play of rows of suspended balls.

Returning to the general exhibition, the existing pictures show a particularly successful solution to the T8 layout: a structural grid for the glazed entrance, in which the 'T' and the '8' are cut out on an opaque background, creating a play of 'breakthroughs' and dynamically projected shadows. In some ways, this approach conjures up the photographic effects that Huber sought in the darkroom by superimposing images, shifting and projecting the shadows of objects. It also recalls the graphic results of the technique that distinguished many of his works in those years based on running colour films out of register. An exciting find in

opposite top
8th Milan Triennale
exhibition design, 1947

opposite bottom
Angelo Bianchetti and
Cesare Pea with Max
Huber
**Concorso a premi per la
casa (Home design
competition)**
advertising stand, 8th Milan
Triennale, 1947

**8th Milan Triennale
(Interior Design Section)**
exhibition design, 1947

top
L'Incubo (The Nightmare)
opera set design, Teatro La Fenice, Venice, 1948

bottom
Achille and Pier Giacomo Castiglioni with Max Huber
Il Giornale Radio (Radio News)
exhibition design, XV Mostra Nazionale della Radio (15th National Radio Exhibition), Palazzo dell'Arte, Milan, 1948

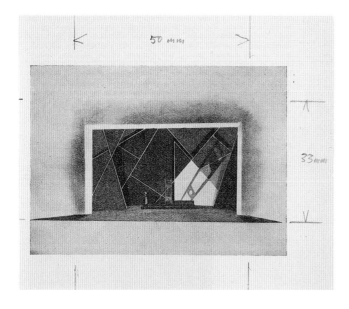

the archives is a sort of photographic report of his works on display, which reveals considerable attention paid to the search for a photographic angle.

We have said that the exhibition 'Arte astratta e concreta' dates from the same period. Huber, who was mainly an exhibiting artist, was also involved in organizing the exhibition. 'The organization, exhibition design and presentation were developed with remarkable finesse by the architect Lanfranco Bombelli Tiravanti, assisted by Max Huber. The architects Elena Berrone and Franca Helg also contributed',[16] wrote Gillo Dorfles in a long critique of the exhibition published in *Domus* in January 1947. No records enable us to pinpoint Huber's exact contribution. However, the lightness of the decor, which consisted of a simple, paper-wrapped tubular-metal structure that created modular, virtual walls for the display of the works, is certainly very similar to the new typographical-composition principles of the Swiss school. The compositional language of the design blends well with the artistic themes proposed by many of the Concrete artists, especially Swiss ones such as Bill and Huber himself.

Also in 1947 Huber undertook two projects for the Fiera di Milano (Milan Trade Fair). They involved the architects Franco Albini and Giancarlo de Carlo and were for the pigment and paint hall in the Ducotone pavilion and the scientific research hall in the Montecatini pavilion.

In 1948, Huber and the BPR group of architects (Belgiojoso, Peressutti and Rogers), for whom the young Swiss architect Stöff Bon was working, participated in the design of the Terni pavilion for the Fiera di Milano. Notable is Huber's graphic involvement in the decision to use an industrial stencil for the lettering on large canvases stretched between tubular-metal structures. These stand out as terse and modern compared with the many graphic signs on the large nearby pavilions, still closely bound to the pedantic and rhetorical formulae of the recent past.

Achille and Pier Giacomo
Castiglioni with Max Huber
and Erberto Carboni
RAI Pavilion
exhibition design, Fiera di
Milano, 1948

Meeting the Castiglioni Brothers, 1948

In 1948, Huber received two more major opportunities to play with three-dimensional space. His acquaintance with the music critic Roberto Leydi (who was to become a great friend and admirer) brought him into contact with the composer Ferdinando Ballo, for whom he designed the set of the opera *L'Incubo*, staged at the Teatro La Fenice in Venice for the 11th International Festival of Contemporary Music.

In the same year, Huber started to work with Achille and Pier Giacomo Castiglioni, with whom he embarked upon a long and productive collaboration, one of the most interesting and significant in the history of exhibition design in Italy and abroad. Their first joint achievement was a section of the XV Mostra Nazionale della Radio (15th National Radio Exhibition), curated overall by the Castiglioni brothers, who asked Huber to lay out the communication panels for the zone devoted to 'Il Giornale Radio' (The Radio News Bulletin). The following year, based on their successful combination of affinities, they worked together on the design of an exhibition on the development of radio-broadcasting in Italy in the new RAI Pavilion (Radio Audizioni Italiane-Italian Radio Broadcasts) created by the Castiglioni brothers at the 27th Fiera di Milano and, almost in conjunction, the general design for the XVI Mostra Nazionale della Radio e Televisione (16th National Radio and Television Exhibition) at Palazzo dell'Arte in Milan.

The design project for the Fiera pavilion also bore the name of Erberto Carboni, a famous exhibition- and coordinated-graphics designer. The 'Carboni style' was one of the most sought after at the time due to his exuberant signs and spectacular settings, as well as the speed and creativity with which he worked. According to Achille Castiglioni it was Carboni, well connected in RAI circles, who had backed the inclusion of the young Castiglioni brothers along with his brilliant Swiss friend Huber, whom he had met in the early 1940s at the Studio Boggeri. The exhibition design project produced by the Castiglioni

bottom and opposite
bottom
Achille and Pier Giacomo
Castiglioni with Max Huber
**XVI Mostra Nazionale
della Radio (16th National
Radio Exhibition)**
exhibition design, Palazzo
dell'Arte, Milan, 1949

opposite top
**XVI Mostra Nazionale
della Radio (16th National
Radio Exhibition)**
exhibition panel, Palazzo
dell'Arte, Milan, 1949
dimensions unknown

brothers with Huber's assistance was lightweight, pared-down and dynamic, and played on the fact that it would be seen from the large 'window' on the upper floor, looking down on the public exhibition spaces. Castiglioni said that Carboni liked the project, but, worried that it was perhaps too economical, suggested adding some extra decor. This led to the idea of including a reproduction of Alexander the Great's horn, a fine and somewhat enigmatic object, as testimony to humankind's first attempt to cast voice over distance. It was, however, the sinusoid of the Herz wave, suspended from the ceiling against a background showing the outlines of the various continents, that best conveyed the effect of the inward and outward communication in the exhibition space. In this case, Huber went along with the ideas of the Castiglioni brothers while Carboni carved out specific, predominantly graphic areas for himself. These included the panel placed at the entrance, which became a sort of publicity poster for the occasion. Prominently featuring Carboni's famous RAI logo at its centre, it portrayed the face of a woman with her mouth half open as if singing, overlaid with concentric waves that expanded out in a spiral. This produced a surreal and exciting visual effect similar to Alfred Hitchcock's hypnotic images.

The Castiglioni brothers and Huber created a stronger design, in terms of integrated graphics and architecture, for the presentation of RAI's radio programmes on the grand staircase at Palazzo dell'Arte. Long, two-sided graphic and photographic panels were allowed to fall freely from the high ceiling and intercept the staircase like two-dimensional pillars at several heights and positions, creating the effect of information raining down harder and harder as people climbed to the upper floor. Here, they experienced the visual impact of coloured signs, photographs and short messages, giving a musical sense of rhythm and sound as well as imparting information. Another room in the same exhibition contained an aerial system of panels and lights,

showing the prodigious innovations of television technology. Huber interpreted or perhaps even initiated this lightweight, elegant display system, illustrating the story with great graphic rigour. He sought to construct an archigraphic interpretation of space with the aid of a female face (like that of a TV presenter), reproduced on a large scale and appearing in several forms (striped, high-contrast, fading-out and so on) in imitation of different television signals.

The series of radio and television exhibitions continued and, in 1950, again with the Castiglioni brothers, Huber embarked on a strange and elegant tribute (not without a hint of irony) to Carboni's graphic gestures. For the section entitled 'Channel Three's First Seven Evenings' he invented seven splendidly vivacious plastic shapes, unmistakably based on Carboni's famous abstract figures, which rhythmically blended images, words and coloured signs.

Huber and Carboni's collaborative work was again fused with that of the Castiglioni brothers for another exhibition design in the RAI pavilion at the 29th Milan Fair in 1951. The theme of the design was RAI's 'Channel Three' i.e. its cultural programmes; and the graphic sign of a segmented spiral, based on a rotated square (a recurrent theme in Huber's artistic research), became the generating element in the pavilion.

A book on the complete works of the Castiglioni brothers lists Huber as the co-designer, with the Castiglioni brothers, of the XXVIII Mostra Nazionale della Radio e Televisione, but there is no trace of this in the Huber archives; nor is there any recognizable sign of his intervention in the photographs published in the book.[17]

From Landmark to Industrial Design, 1950–4

Meanwhile, in 1950, the architect Carlo Pagani had asked Huber to design the logo for the renovated department store La Rinascente. The famous 'IR' logo, which was adopted on an architectural scale outside the building in

left
Max Huber's graphic works for La Rinascente
exhibition panel, Sala delle arti dell'estetica industriale, Fiera di Milano, c. 1955
dimensions unknown

right
La Rinascente: Confezioni Elle Erre ('L R' Collection)
window display design, Milan, c. 1950

opposite
Ludovico Barbiano di Belgiojoso and Enrico Peressutti (BPR) with Max Huber
La forma dell'utile (The Shape of Useful Things)
exhibition design, 9th Milan Triennale, 1951

Piazza del Duomo in Milan, was to become an important archigraphic sign for the nascent city of design. From then on, this prestigious store in the centre of the city became known to many as 'la erre' (literally meaning 'the "R"'). The company later adopted the nickname for one of its clothing ranges 'Elle Erre' (which spells out the name of the letters 'L' and 'R'), for which Huber also created the advertising. In those years, along with a large number of architect and graphic-artist friends such as Steiner, Bruno Munari, Roberto Sambonet and others, Huber amused himself with the invention of window displays for La Rinascente, which always combined extraordinary materials with innovative graphic solutions. In 1951, Peressutti and Belgiojoso of the BBPR group (the third party, Rogers, was busy working on another exhibition design with Gregotti and Stoppino, but Franco Buzzi Ceriani, then still a student, was assisting them) asked Huber to help create the exhibition entitled 'La forma dell'utile (Industrial Design)' (Useful forms (Industrial Design)), part of the 9th Milan Triennale. This is remembered as the first post-war exhibition devoted to the theme of industrial design. BPR's proposal was to arrange the objects on low benches while the overall spatial solution was to hook photographic panels from a light reticular structure, a network of cables stretched between ceiling and floor. Brass balls placed at the nodal points where the cables intersected were suspended in mid-air by this weave. When Huber was called in, the project had already been finalized but he was asked to work on the general graphics as well as to create a 'symbolic object-sculpture' linked to the exhibition theme, which would be placed at the entrance to the exhibition. A notable part of the ensemble was a large, concave panel, bearing an unframed abstract-surreal photograph of metal balls photographed on overlapping glass shelves so that they appeared to be flying, an impression that was aided by the background shadows, probably elaborated by Huber. It was used as the backing for two quotations, one from Adolph Loos, the other from Henry van de Velde, inserted into a pair of

'perforated' bubbles in the photograph. He also suggested a lightweight structural solution for the panels suspended between the cables, 'because they would flex, being made out of lightweight plywood. In the end, they were stiffened with rear strips'.[18] The introductory object-sculpture made of plaster on a metal structure is also interesting – half Carboni-style spectacle (an elegant artistic exercise that created a strong focal point) and half metaphorical construction alluding to the subject of industrial design. Huber explained: 'it may remind you of the handles on the Olivetti typewriters, but also parts of machines tools, such as a drill. A mechanical object with no specific reference. One part, for instance, resembles a ruling-pen.'[19]

The presence in the Huber archives of two pictures of the Movil hall designed by the Castiglioni brothers in 1953 for the Montecatini pavilion would suggest Huber's involvement, although this is not confirmed by further documentation. Given these pictures, his main contribution was apparently the design of the glass cases, which played on a composition of geometric and aerial elements illustrating the properties of Movil man-made yarn. Huber's collaboration in another two projects by the Castiglioni brothers dates from the same year, according to the Castiglioni archives: the design for the RAI pavilion at the 31st Fiera di Milano, with Carboni, and the RAI stand at the 19th Mostra Nazionale della Radio e Televisione. Although his influence is hard to see in the former, it appears more clearly in the latter. However, there is no trace of these projects in the Huber archives or in his biographies.

In 1954, Huber found himself involved in an interesting venture with the architects Carlo Mollino, Franco Campo and Carlo Graffi – the design of the ENI-SNAM pavilion at the Fiera di Milano. The fluid and dynamic unfolding of the exhibition, marked by the irrepressible, expressive language of Mollino and friends, prompted Huber to lend a voice to this complex play of structural grids, fragments and collages. This gave rise to an intersection of graphic, photographic and luminous pieces that are better described as an early

Deconstructivist assembly prototype than a use of Constructivist language. The broken, luminous line created with neon lights seems to be one of Huber's first experiments involving artistically designed lines of light, to which he later returned. In those years, this idea was being proposed in Lucio Fontana's Spatialism, as in the famous entrance to the 9th Milan Triennale of 1951 designed by Luciano Baldessari and Marcello Grisotti, where one of the artist's famous luminous cirrus clouds, created with neon tubes, hung resplendent in the air.

The Compasso d'oro was first awarded in the year 1954, having Huber among its winners. He won it not for a graphic project but for a waterproof plastic translucent sheet, put into production as a curtain for showers or exteriors and featuring a decorative, informal, almost gestural motif. It was an everyday object in a new material ennobled by a playful and informal design that could be used as a versatile partition, shelter or covering.

Aerial Objects, Chinese Shadows and Shifts, 1955–8

In 1955, Huber resumed his collaboration with the Castiglioni brothers on the project for the ENI pavilion at the International Petroleum Exhibition, held in Naples. Huber's hand is visible in several areas of this project, starting with the communication trellis placed outside the pavilion. Although this was certainly the work of the Castiglioni brothers, the composition of aerial elements conveys a graphic montage that closely resembles Huber's spatial work, and we know that the Castiglionis worked closely with Huber on their projects. That Huber took a photograph of this communication structure at least shows his satisfaction with the result of the aerial design. Inside was a magnificent play of Chinese shadows on the illuminated rear walls, created by the Castiglioni brothers. Huber must have been delighted to work on its graphic component, which took the form of large, skilfully composed backdrops. Superimposed photographs (in keeping with the finest school of objective photography) were combined with graphic elements revealing Huber's artistic research into pure intersecting geometric figures (circles and squares).

In 1955, Huber continued his collaboration with the Castiglioni brothers for the RAI stand in the RAI pavilion at the 33rd Fiera di Milano and the general exhibition design, as well as a stand for the 21st Mostra della Radio e della Televisione. The relationship with the Castiglioni brothers and the AGIP-ENI group was maintained in Milan at the 1956 Fiera di Milano. This time, Huber laid out large graphic panels like a huge book and introduced some 'scenographic-sculptural' inventions consisting of clusters of molecules suspended in a nocturnal setting created by the Castiglioni brothers.

The same year saw the design of the Imballaggio Hall for the ANIIGCT pavilion (Associazione Nazionale Italiana Industrie Grafiche Cartotecniche e Trasformatrici) at the 34th Fiera di Milano. Here, the Castiglioni brothers worked with considerable clarity on two communication levels. The first was from the floor up to the height of a person, with orthogonal, vertical partitions in natural plywood, freely organizing the large open space. The second was at a higher level, suspended above the first, played out through a complex system of luminous panels of various shapes: large diffusers made from rings of white paper stretched between neon lights.

Huber offered a careful interpretation of this elegant play of opaque and luminous partitions, using large, full-bodied capital letters on the wooden panels, and light but graphically defined capital letters on the diffusers. In the same year, and again with the Castiglioni brothers, he also contributed to the design of the 22nd Mostra della Radio e della Televisione at Palazzo dello Sport in Milan.

The Castiglioni brothers asked Huber to make another major graphic contribution to the stepped roof they designed for the ENI pavilion at the

Fiera di Milano in 1958. The object was to create a large, corporate-communication facade with a staggered front, hence playing on an image that changed constantly with the point of observation. Only from a distance of four metres from the entrance could the graphics on the facade be read properly. Otherwise, a constant shifting of the rising bands that were aligned with each step produced an abstract and dynamic perception of the signs.

Pinball Aesthetics, Disproportion, Technicolour Effects and the Revival Game, 1959–60

The same year marked another pyrotechnical game invented by Huber that perfectly matched the Castiglioni brothers' cavalier spirit. He designed a twenty-five-metre long facade resembling a huge pinball machine for the RAI stand at the 24th Mostra della Radio e della Televisione, the theme of which was the new radio broadcasting service. The visual impact was strong and the message was immediate, and perhaps unscrupulous. The *Rassegna pubblicitaria* issue of May 1959 read: 'Both the design of the surroundings and the graphics intentionally lack all finesse of composition, taste, materials and colour, something always found in the most modern and refined exhibition designs. The large wall features only a play of coloured light and of movement, which draws visitors into a light-filled, liberating and almost fun environment reminiscent of the halls where young people crowd around pinball machines and juke-boxes.'[20]

In 1959, Huber made a graphic design contribution to four exhibition proposals by the Castiglioni brothers. His intervention was minimal in the case

of the RAI pavilion at the 37th Fiera di Milano: a graphic panel inserted into a number of posters created by graphic-artist friends (B Munari, A Steiner, G Illiprandi, P Tovaglia and H Weibl, among others) on the theme 'A Radio Invitation', which the Castiglioni brothers used in the internal tiered gallery. He made a more significant contribution to the Autovox pavilion at the 25th Mostra Nazionale della Radio e della Televisione; here, with the Castiglioni brothers, he created an ideal archigraphic episode by printing 'Autovox' full height on a close-packed fence of slats, which virtually enclosed the stand and were arranged vertically and side on, so as to look transparent when viewed sideways at a ninety-degree angle and solid if seen from a different angle. As with the stepped ENI pavilion, Huber played on the dynamic perception of the lettering, which appears and disappears on the side of the stand according to the position of the viewer.

The same year saw a masterpiece by the Castiglioni brothers and Huber, the Paint hall in the Montecatini pavilion of the 37th Fiera di Milano. The Castiglioni brothers prepared the blank, or rather transparent, pages on which Huber laid out a colour manual. 'The design', reads the project report drawn up by the Castiglionis, 'was created without recourse to great volumetric and plastic compositions … with just one colour (white) so as to highlight the display material, which revolved around its own colours, as much as possible'.[21] Thus the colour white was chosen for the receptacle, which was left entirely undecorated. Inside was a totally dematerialised design consisting of a sequence of screens, each made of four panes of toughened glass, inserted into minimal floor bases and held in equilibrium by special clamps linked by metal cables anchored to the walls. The first of the six screens bore the word 'VERNICI' (paints) in large letters and this became the title of the exhibition. It was followed by the various Duco paint ranges, which Huber presented to great technicolour effect in graphic plays of form and colour; these blended together joyously thanks to the transparent backing panels.

The Splügen Bräu beer stand was designed in 1959 for the Fiera di Milano, and linked to an important 1960 creation, the Splügen Bräu beer-house restaurant on corso Europa in Milan. In both cases, Huber's work consisted in playing, almost as if in musical counterpoint, on the stylistic 'phrases' developed ironically by the Castiglioni brothers: the logos and names of the various beers became light, coloured notes in the tangle of modern and strangely outmoded 'voices' assembled by the Castiglioni brothers. The beer-house restaurant on corso Europa produced a highly worthwhile result, considered one of the most interesting episodes in the renewal of Italian architecture at the beginning of the 1960s. The factors that contributed towards this achievement certainly include the large, vertical, luminous sign on the exterior, designed by Huber, which covers the block containing the service entrance linking the old adjacent house to the new beer house building.

The Plastics hall in the Montecatini pavilion of the 38th Fiera di Milano was also designed in 1960; this time, Huber worked with G Illiprandi in a communicational composition consisting of words and objects displayed in open glass cases, designed, as was the whole exhibition, by the Castiglioni brothers.

From a 'Graphic Wall' to Logos on an Urban Scale, 1961–3

In 1961, a large exhibition entitled 'Italia 61' was held in Turin to celebrate the hundredth anniversary of Italian unification. Huber, along with other leading contemporary Italian graphic designers and artists (including Tovaglia and Melotti), was asked to compose his own visual interpretation of the powerful play of metal volumes in Gio Ponti's general exhibition design. His task was to introduce visitors to the pavilion given over to the 'evolution of form in advertising'. Huber made some decidedly archigraphic choices for the two entrance and exit facades. He inserted large graphic panels into the vertical apertures in the modular grid of cladding panels designed by Ponti; these

projected like walls from the tilted plane of the pavilion and were placed at right angles to the floor. The design of the facade was completed with the long, luminous word 'pubblicità' (advertising), positioned vertically along the plane of the tilted axis, on a narrower module. The vertical joints were disguised at the top by a panel that was the same width as the exhibition design modules and by a cylindrical advertising display laid along that axis at the bottom. Except for the lettering '1961' and the lively, almost musical, typographical composition of the word 'advertising' repeated in five languages, the other facade looked like a pure abstract composition made of light and colour. The off-register panel strip was covered with a three-dimensional, triangular-section measuring stick, the measuring effect being created by a sequence of coloured bands along the sides. The three-dimensional expansion of the facade was mainly achieved via a luminous play of large planes projecting from its tilted line (this time laid horizontally and parallel to the ground), made of coloured neon tubes that lit up in intermittent sequences. Huber attributed great importance to the effect of the reflections produced by the stainless steel 'Enduro-Fiat' surfaces chosen by Ponti to construct the imposing, fortress-like pavilions inside the huge Palazzo del Lavoro, which itself was designed by Pier Luigi Nervi as a receptacle for this great event. This interest in reflections is also clear from the pictures of two rare project models that Huber made to study certain solutions. The models differ in all but a few details from the final result but he adopts an interesting play of *objets trouvés* in these initial suggestions.

In 1961, Huber created graphics for the Castiglioni brothers' work on the entrance to the Montecatini pavilion at the Fiera di Milano, the scientific research hall. A typically Castiglioni play of mirrors multiplied a large photomontage, edited by Huber, containing words arranged directly on the mirrors. The whole creates an exciting sense of radially expanding space, in which the mirror on the left imitates a window placed at the centre of a large staircase, to which text has been applied.

Also worth mentioning is the 1962 polypropylene section in the Montecatini pavilion at the 40th Fiera di Milano, created by Huber and the young H Waibl for the Castiglioni brothers; and, in the same year, the Autovox stand at the Salone dell'Auto in Turin, again with the Castiglioni brothers.

A highly significant 1962 venture was that undertaken with the industrial designer Rodolfo Bonetto to design a face for the Sfericlock alarm clock manufactured by Borletti, which won the Compasso d'oro in 1964. In two particularly interesting versions of the face, Huber experimented with dynamically perceived signs, whereby increasingly longer hands or an increasing number of balls communicated the passing hours.

An unusual archigraphic feat was achieved in 1963 with the creation of the sign for the chain of stores known as Supermarket. The carefully studied extension of the top of the 'S' turned the logo (originally designed in 1958–9) into a familiar landmark. So effective was this sign in the city of Milan that people soon started referring to the supermarket chain as 'Esselunga' (which literally translates as 'Long "S"'), a name that later became official.

The Search for a New Narrative Language, 1963–6

Between 1963 and 1964, Huber participated in two Castiglioni brothers' designs whose innovative narrative language makes them milestones in the

left
Achille and Pier Giacomo
Castiglioni with Max Huber
**Vie d'acqua da Milano al
mare (Waterways from
Milan to the Sea)**
exhibition design, Palazzo
Reale, Milan, 1963

right and opposite
Achille and Pier Giacomo
Castiglioni with Max Huber
Montecatini Pavilion
exhibition design, Fiera di
Milano, 1964

history of exhibition architecture. These were the projects for the exhibition 'Vie d'acqua da Milano al mare' (Waterways from Milan to the Sea) at Palazzo Reale in Milan in 1963, and the design of the Montecatini pavilion entitled 'Developments in the Petrochemical Industry Seen Through the Story of an Oil Drop' at the 42nd Fiera di Milano in 1964. It is curious to note that the same communicational model was adopted for these exhibitions, one cultural and the other commercial. 'Both the "Vie d'acqua da Milano al mare" exhibition', wrote the Castiglioni brothers, 'and the design for the Montecatini pavilion in 1964, … shared the same problem: how to illustrate an idea to the public. How do you establish a connection with the observer that allows for the communication of concepts, data, notions and problems that can rarely be articulated through "objects" as exhibition aids?'[22] In the first case, Huber entered into the direct and exciting narrative spirit created by the Castiglioni brothers with simple 'poor' elements (interestingly, this is similar to the approach of the Italian Arte Povera or 'Poor Art' movement of the time). He also applied texts to the work planks that constituted the shell of the design, a work-in-progress communication, created using stencilled letters similar to those seen on freight crates. Many of the images were also serigraphed directly onto the untreated wooden planks in a Brutalist manner. Huber had an opportunity to test several different communication techniques in the Montecatini pavilion project, conceived as a route where visitors could experiment with different sensations in themed, theatre-like sets – from moving, luminous graphics to photographic montages – all elaborated on a scale suited to the architectural dimension.

In 1964, the Castiglioni brothers also designed the RAI pavilion at the 42nd Fiera di Milano, placing all the pavilion's perimeter walls, painted white, at Huber's disposal to exercise his masterly archigraphic sensitivity. He saturated the surfaces with huge letters in several shades of grey, spelling out the theme of the year: *Dieci anni di televisione in Italia* (Ten Years of Italian Television). A photographed detail of this design, a lower-case letter 'e', taller than a person, bearing the date 1964 and resting on the floor, brings to mind the work of Robert Venturi in the United States during those years, when large-scale advertising in American metropolises quickly led to the development of

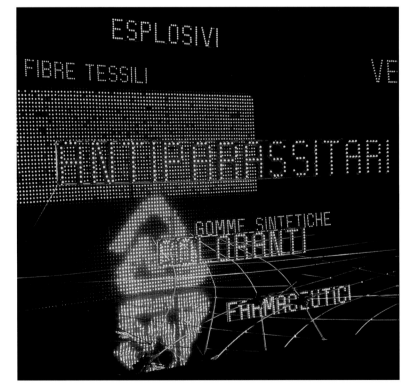

his concept of Pop Architecture, often playing on the impact of the archigraphic sign.

Remaining on the subject of huge lettering that blends with exhibition design solutions, Huber made an effective proposal in the same year, for the Autovox stand, designed with the Castiglioni brothers for the 30th Mostra della Radio e della Televisione. A large, tilted surface placed above the stands became a road with passing vehicles reduced to carcasses, to which a few elements (car radios, wheels and other strange everyday objects) were attached; the graphics were based on street signs, such as pedestrian-crossing stripes and the starting lights of a grand prix race.

1966 saw the Montecatini pavilion design for the exhibition 'Chimica: agricoltura più ricca' (Chemistry: Richer Agriculture), a project by the Castiglioni brothers with Huber's graphics. 'Teamwork, consistent colour, no graphics for their own sake, measured intervention, attention only to precise and essential insertion', was Huber's comment on the project in *Design Italia* of that year. 'I did without the external placard, no views of chemical plants and fertile fields. I restricted myself to just a "title". On the inside, I rejected the usual didactic panels and wanted the names of the various halls written directly on the walls; only once did I resort to a glazed partition. I adopted the same criteria for the layout of the exhibition cases, the so-called "displays", so there was no emphasis in the explanatory captions for each display.'[23]

Synthetic Checks on the Story's Complexity, 1967–91

In 1967, Huber returned to the Montecatini pavilion with the Castiglioni brothers, for 'Chimica = un domani + sicuro' (Chemistry = a Safer Future); here, we see another exhibition design masterpiece, in a sense the *summa* of all the Castiglioni brothers' experimentation in the Montecatini pavilion over a period of fifteen years. In previous designs, the Castiglioni brothers had achieved a refined and innovative result through episodic narration that produced a continuing alienating effect. They now felt the need to simplify the story and, as in the history of modern theatre stage-craft, play on the negation and the constantly unfolding ambiguities of the constructed space. Thus the pavilion was entirely emptied out, its full size accentuated by

opposite top
Achille and Pier Giacomo
Castiglioni with Max Huber
Montecatini Pavilion
exhibition design, Fiera di
Milano, 1967

opposite bottom
Achille and Pier Giacomo
Castiglioni with Max Huber
and Giancarlo Illiprandi
RAI Pavilion
exhibition design, Fiera di
Milano, 1964

right
**Montedison Group
Pavilion (formerly
Montecatini Pavilion)**
drawing and detail of neon
sculpture, Fiera di Milano,
1969
dimensions unknown

reverberating glossy white walls, floor and ceiling. However, as always, there was a trick – a very low ceiling, just two metres above the floor, which gave the effect of dilated space. Large recesses were incorporated in the ceiling, however, which looked like empty boxes. Huber acted skilfully in these suspended rooms with hypnotic coloured portrayals against a dark background: a huge anatomical figure conveyed the idea of future man as a potentially perfect machine; arrows and colours steered the gaze towards transport projects developed thanks to chemistry; a huge pea pod symbolized a healthier and chemically controlled diet; the house appeared as mass-produced, aggregated cells; clothes were turned into new objects and the sea was portrayed as a goldmine of new resources. At the end of this 'non-route', where visitors were captured 'like moths in the light'[24] by Huber's decorated boxes, they came to the last surprise: a pool of light and reflections that moved up and down thanks to reflecting planes on both ceiling and floor, which endlessly multiplied the images of visitors looking over the parapet, as well as the text panels laid onto them.

Huber's search for a three-dimensional transposition of his graphic (and artistic) language found an unusual opportunity for expression in his work on the Castiglioni project for the Omega shop in Piazza del Duomo in Milan, dated 1968. As well as innovatively placing signs horizontally beneath the intrados of the architrave of the dual-height shop windows, Huber designed a large, aluminium clock-sculpture, featuring luminous digital numbers, which would powerfully impact on the urban space. It employed a play of intersecting spheres and discs, whose two-dimensional design was based on the graphics of an analogue clock face. Its spiral movement was intended to attract the eyes of passers-by, who saw its fulcrum in the half-sphere containing the digital message.

In the same year of 1968 Huber worked for the last time with the Castiglioni brothers, this time on the Montecatini-Edison pavilion at the Fiera di Milano. The most important contribution was the spiral lettering, placed on the large entrance panel, stating the title of that year's exhibition: 'La chimica ci veste' (Chemistry Clothes Us).

At the end of the 1960s, Huber was asked, with his Zurich designer friends Keller+Bachmann, to design the exhibition 'Magie des Papiers' (The Magic of Paper) at the Kunstgewerbemuseum in Zurich. His last work on the former Montecatini pavilion, by this time known as the Montedison Group Pavilion, was in 1969. Working with the architects Corsini and Wiskemann, Huber designed a gigantic fresco for the new slatted aluminium facade encapsulating the old building. The theme of the exhibition, 'L'uomo e la chimica' (Man and Chemistry), inspired him to fill this enormous screen with the faces of men, women and children, mostly smiling; the graphic treatment adopted a photomechanical procedure that turns photographic images into pure graphic signs that can be conveyed in various colours. For the interior, Huber was commissioned to design a sculpture, created using coloured neon lights, based on chemical compositions. Placed in the centre of a long spiral ramp, this became the *fulcrum* around which the display revolved. Yet again, Huber felt the need to bring his artistic research into the communication process. On other occasions, this research resulted in an aluminium mural decoration in the Gondola junior-high school (1981); a broken line of multi-coloured neon lights for the Flos-Arteluce stand designed by Achille Castiglioni for Euroluce in 1984; an aluminium sculpture in the main Ticino Vita building in Breganzona (1984); and a decorative painted aluminium wall in the Unione delle Banche Svizzere building in Lugano (1988). After Pier Giacomo Castiglioni's death in 1969, Huber had the opportunity to collaborate with Achille Castiglioni again on three major designs for the Italian pavilion at the Geneva Fair for Telecom '71, Telecom '75 and Telecom '79. His work for these exhibitions is fitting and efficient but lacks the spark of the previous projects. This time, Castiglioni's design was fairly restrained within a rigorous organizational scheme.

The last exhibition design in which Huber was involved was the exhibition entitled 'Coincidenze' (Coincidences), held in 1991 at the Castelgrande in Bellinzona. Although, officially, this was the final joint venture for Max (Huber) and Cicci (Castiglioni), the design of the Record watch, produced for Alessi in 1989, is perhaps a more significant swansong for these two great friends and designers. Castiglioni wanted a watch that would be easy to read, with a large dial and asked Huber to design the face. Huber chose the most traditional form, with large, highly legible numbers. 'The result', concluded Castiglioni, 'was a watch that was "all face" easy and quick to read, simple and based more on the principle of removing, rather than adding'[25].

Portfolio: Industry (Late Works)

Oscar Braendli and Adriano Olivetti represented the kind of enlightened entrepreneur that emerged in the first half of the twentieth century in Lombardy, although they were active in different spheres. While continuing to preside over their family industries – Olivetti's manufactured typewriters and other office producs; Braendli's manufactured wallpaper and other home furnishings – they were concerned with the all-round economic development and social rebirth of the whole country, not simply seeking personal profit. In addition to this, Olivetti founded the editorial house Edizioni di Comunità in 1946, through which he spread his progressive cultural ideals. Both men were socially committed, educated entrepeneurs whose aesthetic choices bore the same underlying ethos as those of communication designers, writers, musicians and men of the theatre. They were part of an elite that helped to create the rebirth of Italy in the period between 1945 and the first half of the 1960s.

Braendli asked Max Huber to renew the company's image, and he embraced the designer's radical interpretation of product communication. Huber designed a new wallpaper for Braendli named 'Rhythm', which featured the jazz musician Louis Armstrong. Huber also created the graphics used on the company's stands, fully adhering both to the coordinated image and to his own language, based on abstract form and colour research.

He did the same for the specialist journals he designed for Olivetti, in which form and colour prevailed and photographs were transformed into abstract compositional elements within the visual field.

carte da parati

BRÆNDLI

left, opposite bottom left
and opposite right
Brændli
mural, RIMA (Riunione
Italiana Mostre
Arredamento – Italian
Interior Design Exhibitions),
Palazzo dell'Arte, Milan,
c. 1946

opposite top left
Brændli
advertisement, featured in
the back cover of the 8th
Milan Triennale Catalogue,
1947
240 x 225 mm

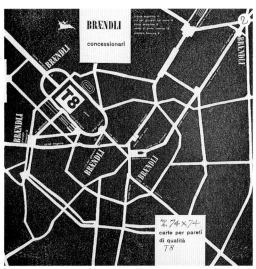

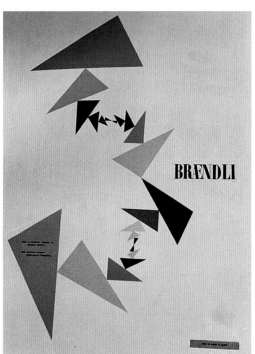

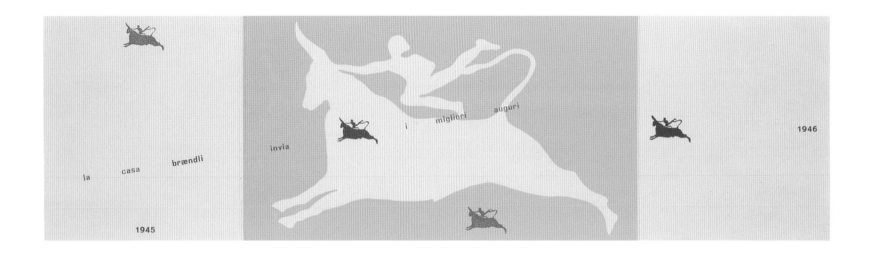

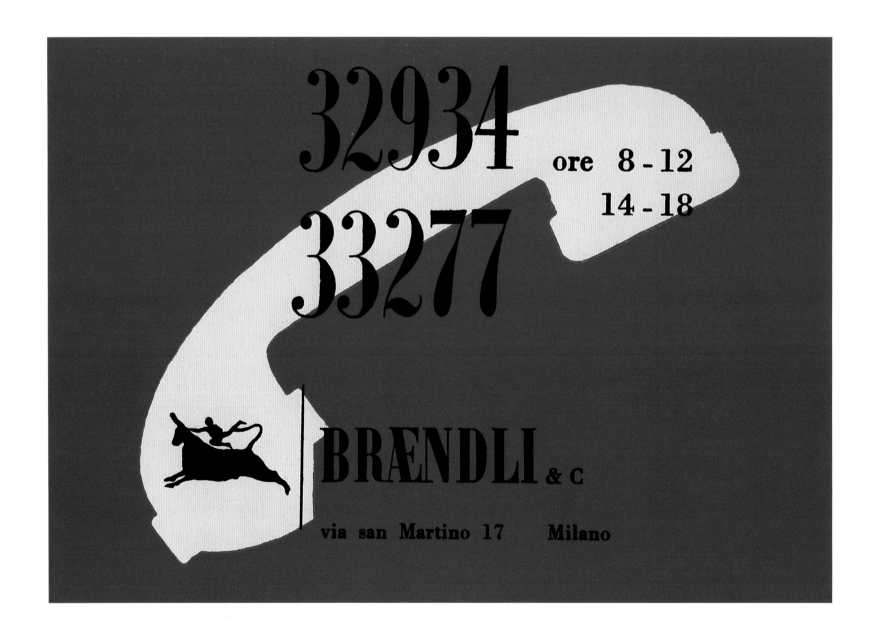

opposite top
Max Huber for Studio
Boggeri
**Christmas Card for
Brændli**
1947
80 x 290 mm

opposite bottom
Brændli
postcard, 1947
110 x 150 mm

Brændli fantasie
catalogue cover, 1947
230 x 230 mm

fantasie

BRÆNDLI

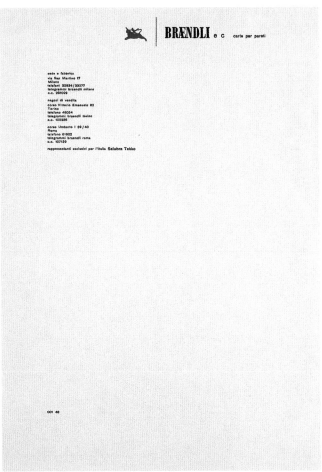

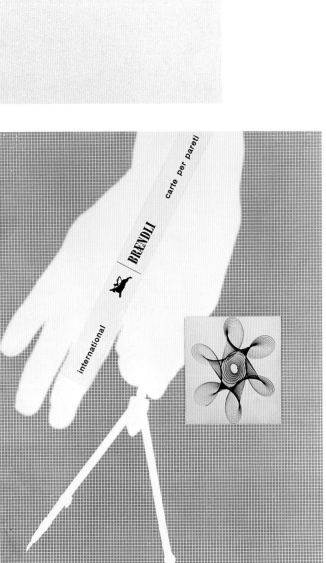

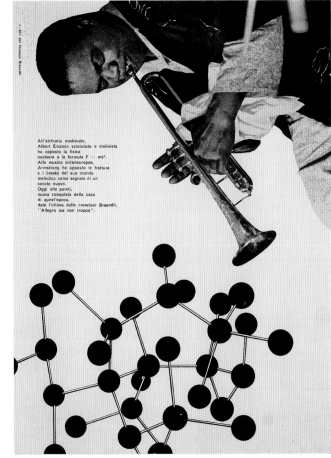

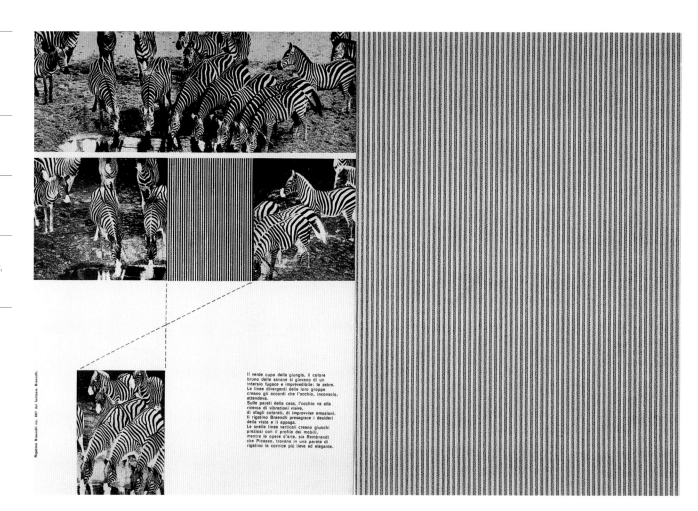

Max Huber for Studio
Boggeri
Olivetti: Studio 42
study for catalogue cover,
1942
325 x 240 mm

carta
carbone

Ing. C. Olivetti & C. S.p.A. Ivrea Italy

carta
carbone

olivetti

carta
carbone

K

carta
carbone

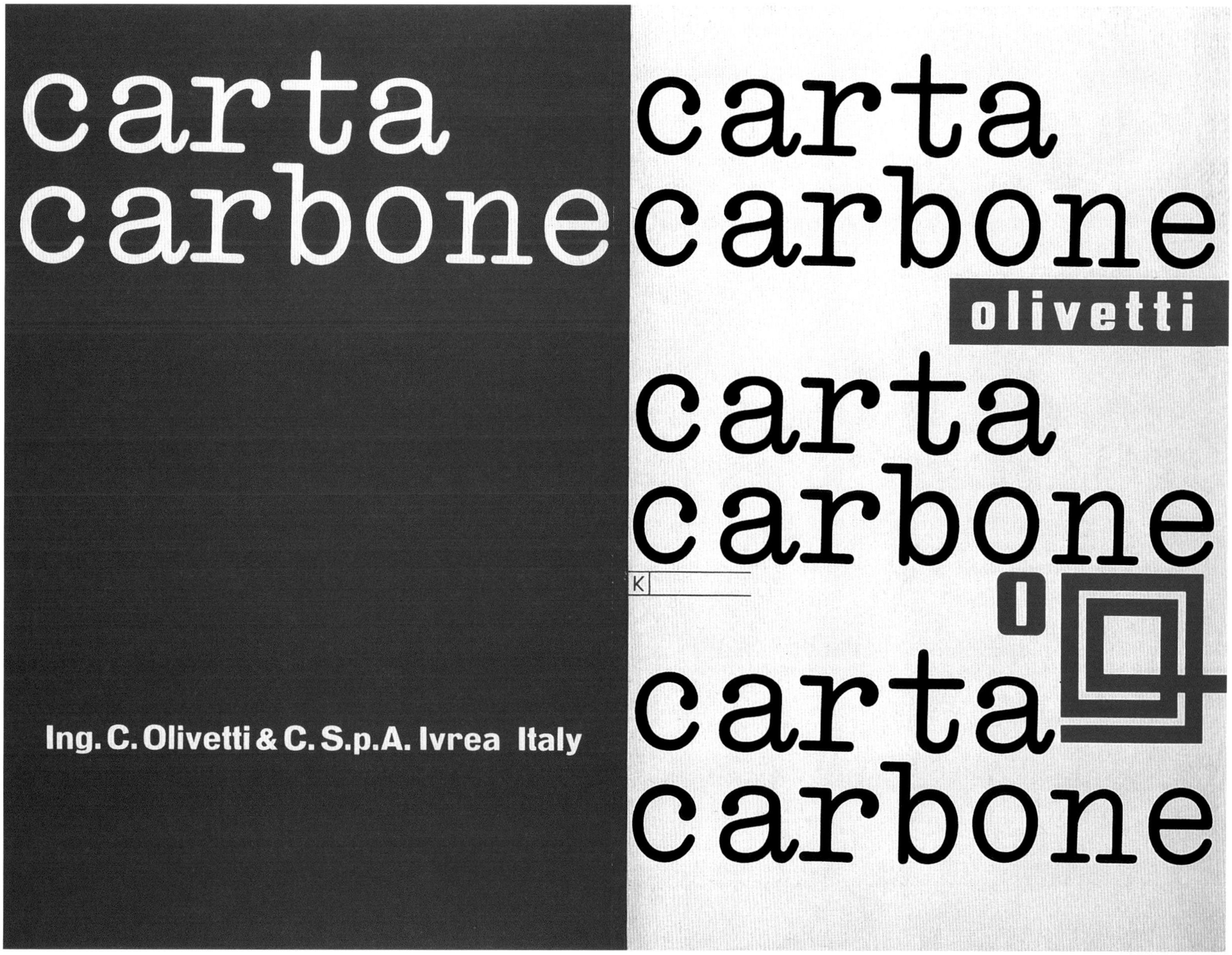

imballaggio

n. 13 luglio ottobre 1952

AETAS
editrice milano

left and opposite
Imballaggio (Packaging)
magazine covers, ETAS,
1952–6
325 x 245 mm

imballaggio

organo ufficiale dell'Istituto Italiano Imballaggio   n. 32   gennaio febbraio 1956

ET|AS   editrice

via mantegna 6   milano   spedizione in abbonamento postale   gruppo quarto

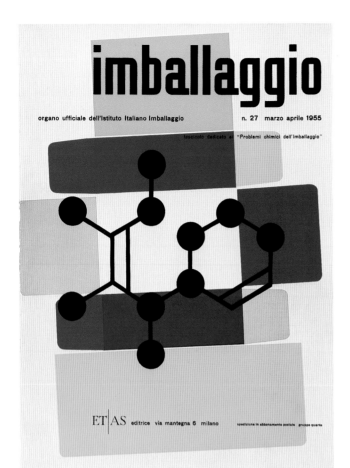

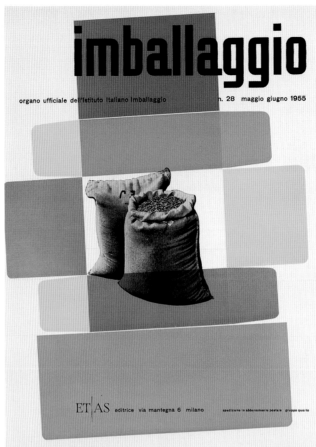

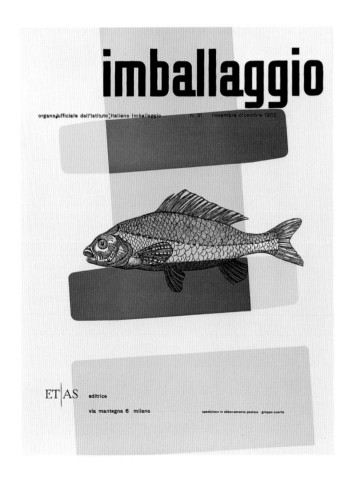

left and opposite
Imballaggio (Packaging)
magazine covers, ETAS,
1955–65
325 x 245 mm

imballaggio

Organo ufficiale dell'Istituto Italiano Imballaggio

anno XII   numero **75**   1961

Macchine e imballaggi per prodotti farmaceutici
Fascicolo speciale

ET|AS   editrice   via mantegna 6   milano   spedizione in abbonamento postale gruppo quarto

interconsult

opposite
Interconsult
brochure cover, 1961
305 x 205 mm

**Rivoluzione Industriale
(Industrial Revolution)**
magazine covers, 1960–1
295 x 210 mm

right and opposite
3M
brochure cover and inside
pages, 1962
190 x 190 mm

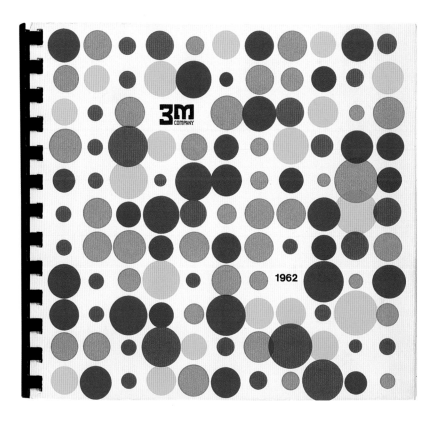

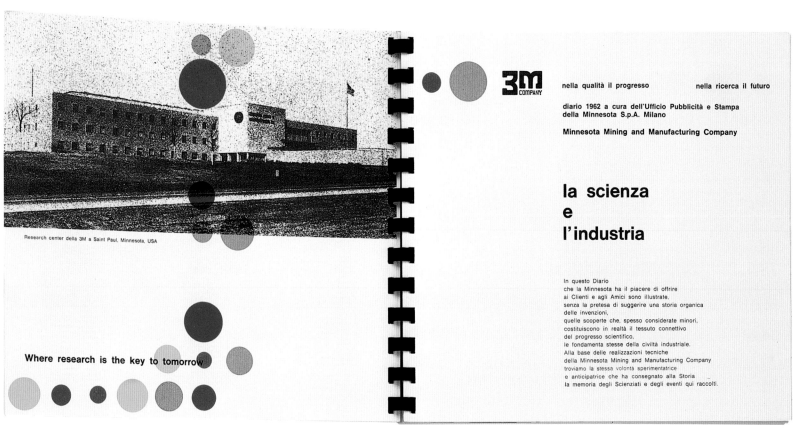

Research center della 3M a Saint Paul, Minnesota, USA

Where research is the key to tomorrow

3M COMPANY

nella qualità il progresso   nella ricerca il futuro

diario 1962 a cura dell'Ufficio Pubblicità e Stampa
della Minnesota S.p.A. Milano

Minnesota Mining and Manufacturing Company

la scienza
e
l'industria

In questo Diario
che la Minnesota ha il piacere di offrire
ai Clienti e agli Amici sono illustrate,
senza la pretesa di suggerire una storia organica
delle invenzioni,
quelle scoperte che, spesso considerate minori,
costituiscono in realtà il tessuto connettivo
del progresso scientifico,
le fondamenta stesse della civiltà industriale.
Alla base delle realizzazioni tecniche
della Minnesota Mining and Manufacturing Company
troviamo la stessa volontà sperimentatrice
e anticipatrice che ha consegnato alla Storia
la memoria degli Scienziati e degli eventi qui raccolti.

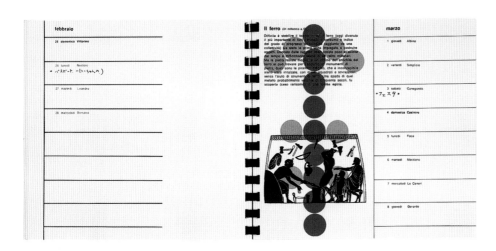

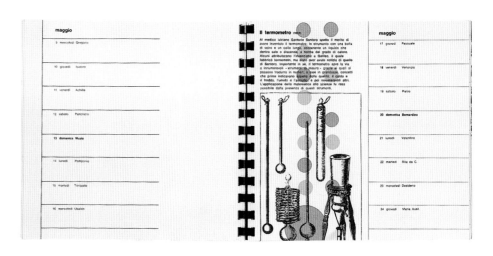

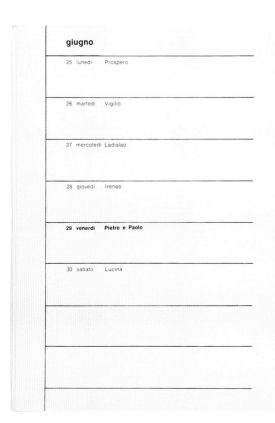

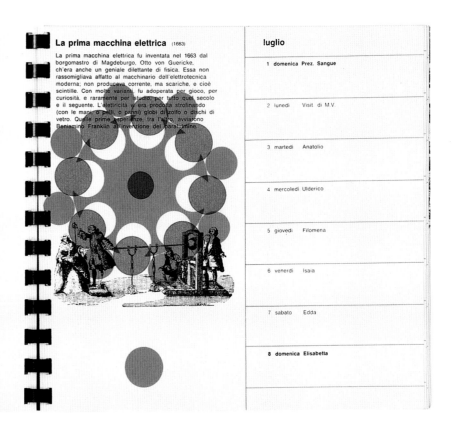

Lemsa
advertisement, 1947
325 x 245 mm

top left
Esso
advertisement, 1956
245 x 170 mm

top right
Gulf Italia
advertisement, 1960
345 x 255 mm

bottom
Supershell Good Mileage Gasoil
logo, 1963

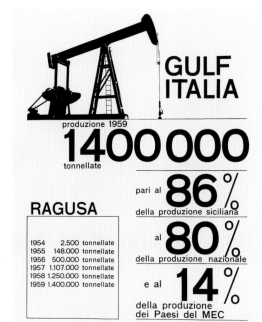

Rows 1 and 2
Albitex
logo and variations, 1961

Row 3
Various logos
Sacill, 1941; Interpol, 1944;
SCEI, 1945; COIN, 1955;
Autovox, 1944

Row 4
Various logos
Furniply, 1959; TEMI, 1960;
Palazi Editori, 1963;
Omniafili, 1963; ASM, 1972

Row 5
Various logos
Habitat, 1980; Ticino Vita,
1980; Milan Triennale, 1985;
Tipo Print, 1988; Seterie
Argenti, 1986

Portfolio: Textile Industry

The postwar economic recovery enabled Italy to diversify its production activities; craft workshops quickly turned into small and medium-sized firms. Local trades permitted the existence of pockets of prosperity thanks to the particular skills of their craftspeople: footwear in Vigevano, steel and metal processing for domestic articles in Omegna, furniture in Brianza, clothing and textiles around Como.

Huber worked for the textile industry from the early 1940s, in Switzerland as well as in Italy. He designed for Bantam and for Borsalino, both hat manufacturers. In his celebrated posters for Borsalino, he used a man's hat revolving in the field of vision, evoking Magritte's Surrealism. It is unclear whether he did so consciously or not; he was, however, familiar with German avant-garde photography and the pictures of Willy Otto Zielke and Albert Renger Patzsch in particular, which removed everyday commodities from their contexts, treating them as pure forms in series. This influence can also be seen in the outlines of shoes that Huber made for window display posters for Bally.

The textile firms Bemberg and Legler represented a breaking away from tradition, especially in terms of the nature of their products: both companies produced new man-made fibres, and primary, geometric forms prevailed in their communication materials, designed by Huber. A circle suggested the cross-section of a fabric roll or was transformed into a spiral; centripetal or centrifugal force often determined the optical centre of the communication. It is not certain whether Huber was fully familiar with the recent theories of perception, but his lucid mind turned every design choice into a demonstration of the need to act on a level of language rather than persuasion.

top
Vanzina Hats
window display poster, 1940
250 x 310 mm

bottom left
Tela cerata (Oilcloth)
study for advertisement,
1939
150 x 220 mm

bottom right
PKZ
window display poster, 1939
870 x 630 mm

Bemberg
GOZZANO

Pubblicazione trimestrale – Anno III · N. 1·2 · 1941·XIX – Sped. Abbon. Postale (Gruppo 4)

Max Huber for Studio Boggeri
Bemberg
magazine cover, 1941
325 x 240 mm

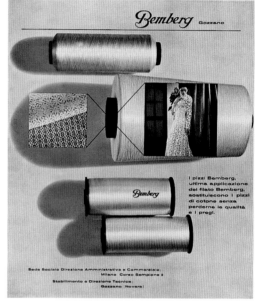

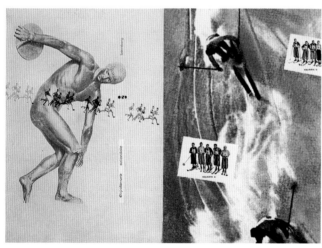

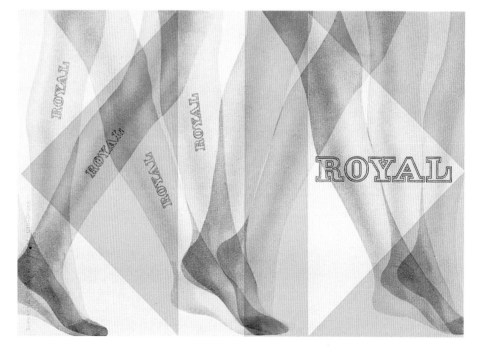

left
Borsalino
advertisement, 1949
320 x 125 mm

right
Borsalino
poster, 1949
1000 x 700 mm

Max Huber

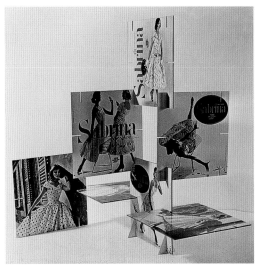

top left
Legler
brochure cover, 1955
205 x 195 mm

top right and centre right
Sabrina Legler
logo and point of sale, 1956

bottom left
Legler
advertisement, 1950s
185 x 360 mm

opposite top
Legler
calendar, 1959
260 x 85 mm

opposite centre
Legler
calendar, 1960
260 x 85 mm

opposite bottom left
Legler Fashion Weekend 1964
leaflet, 1964
300 x 90 mm

opposite bottom right
Hanky Legler
packaging, c. 1950
150 x 300 mm

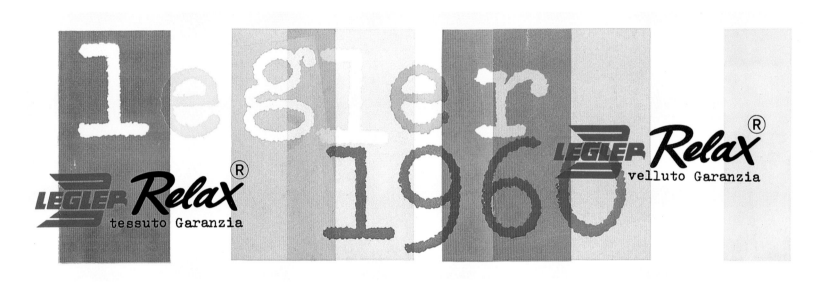

CP/02   O.M.F. PISTOIESI
Doppelkrempel und Eintrommeln für Kammgarn und synthetische Fasern

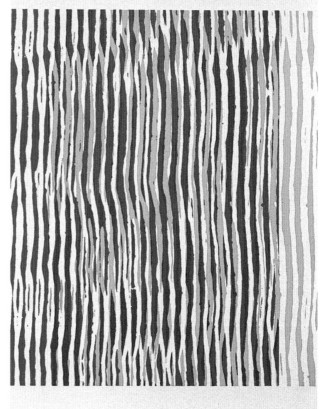

SUPER DRAFTER CDS   OTO MELARA

High draft
intersecting
with incorporated   OTO MELARA

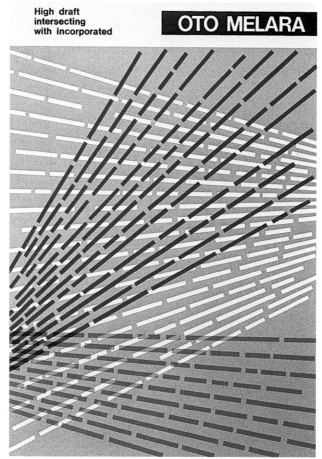

Qualità
da più
di cento anni

GRUPPO TESSILE NIGGELER & KÜPFER

sede amministrativa:
25031 Capriolo / Brescia. telefono (030) 736061

Filature Niggeler & Küpfer spa / Capriolo. Brescia
Tessiture Niggeler & Küpfer spa / Chiari. Brescia
Filatura di Pilzone spa / Pilzone d'Iseo. Brescia
Nuova Manifattura di Breno spa / Ceto. Brescia
Filatura dell'Isonzo spa / Romans d'Isonzo. Gorizia
Dajana spa / Adro. Brescia
Manifattura di Pedrengo spa / Pedrengo. Bergamo

top
Niggeler & Küpfer
advertisement, 1976
310 x 240 mm

bottom left
Niggeler & Küpfer
study for advertisement,
c. 1970s
300 x 210 mm

bottom centre
Niggeler & Küpfer
advertisement, c. 1970
380 x 280 mm

bottom right
Niggeler & Küpfer
logo, 1964

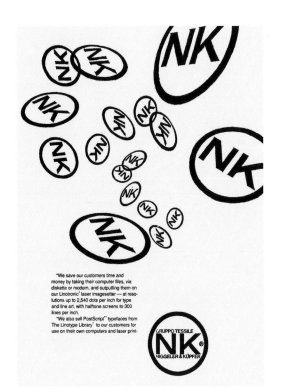

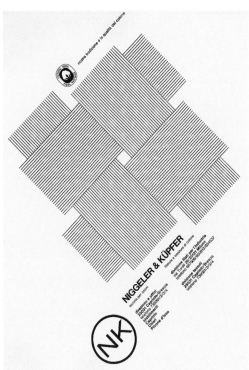

NIGGELER & KÜPFER

società per azioni

direzione e uffici
25031 Capriolo/Brescia
telefono 736061/2/3/4
stabilimenti
Capriolo
Chiari
Pilzone d'Iseo

divisione filati per l'industria
via Turati 26/**20121 Milano**
telefono 667909/650813/654537

divisione tessuti
25031 Capriolo/Brescia
telefono 736061/2/3/4

il marchio e la qualità nella moderna produzione del cotone

top left, bottom right and
opposite
Niggeler & Küpfer
brochure cover and inside
pages, 1976
240 x 310 mm

bottom left
Niggeler & Küpfer
advertisement, c. 1976
300 x 230 mm

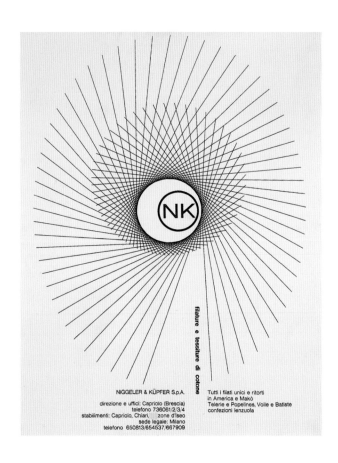

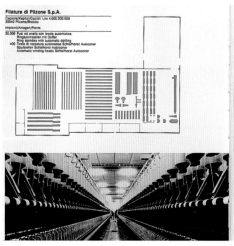

1876
Gualtiero Schmid and Giovanni Niggeler establish the Schmid and Niggeler Company, with head-office in Palazzolo S/Oglio (Brescia).

1888
Gualtiero Schmid retires from the Company and is replaced by Emilio Küpfer.
The Company assumes a last name as Niggeler & Küpfer S.p.A., with head-office in Palazzolo S/Oglio (Brescia).

1890
Niggeler & Küpfer acquires at Chiari (Brescia) a Textile factory powered by hydroenergy and the restructured systems, lodge a spinning mill and a weaving mill for cotton.

1894
Niggeler & Küpfer acquires a mill at Capriolo in the province of Brescia which has very elevated hydropower; this represents the start of the industrial build up which includes the construction of a dam on the river Oglio, with the widening of the old channel, the construction of a hydroplant and of the industrial complex which reaches the potentiality of 60,000 spindles.

1920
The Company from a collective name becomes a liability company.

1955/60
The factories of Capriolo and Chiari are restructurated, remodernised and enlarged; the buildings in Palazzolo are abandoned and the head-office is moved to Capriolo (Brescia).

1963
The new Filatura of Pilzone d'Iseo (Brescia) is constituted for fine counts and is enlarged in 1969, at the end 22,000 spindles are installed.

1969
The Dajana Industria Confezioni Tessili S.p.A. is constituted, located in Adro (Brescia) which manufactures shirts for men and household items.

1970/1975
A new spinning mill for carded yarns is built in Capriolo. The weaving mills are increased

with the construction of a new factory in Mornico al Serio (Bergamo).

1973
The group partecipates, as paritary partner, in the constitution of the Manifattura di Pedrengo S.p.A., located in Pedrengo (Bergamo), finalized for the production of carded yarns.

1975/76
The Filatura dell'Isonzo S.p.A. is constituted, located in Romans d'Isonzo (Gorizia) where a new "open end" spinning mill is built.

1976/80
The Filatura of Breno is incorporated into "Nuova Manifattura di Breno S.p.A.", in which the Niggeler & Küpfer holds the majority of shares, and starts a programme of restructuration which includes the doubling of the spinning plant.

1978/86
In Capriolo the output of the hydroelectric plant is increased; the spinning plant for carded yarn in Capriolo is renovated with the installation of modern open end "Autocoro Schlafhorst".
In Chiari starts a complete remodernation and enlargement of the weaving plant.

1980
The Niggeler & Küpfer S.p.A. is changed into an Industrial Holding.
The plants of Capriolo, Chiari, Mornico and Pilzone are brought to the followings companies:

Capriolo and Hydroelectric plant
Filature Niggeler & Küpfer S.p.A.

Pilzone
Filatura of Pilzone S.p.A.

Chiari and Mornico
Tessiture Niggeler & Küpfer S.p.A.

1985
Between the companies of the groups, a consortium is constituted for the common utilization of the own produced electrical energy; also the construction of the hydroplant of Castel Montecchio, begins. The studies, for the realization of the project for the hydroelectrical plants of Valpaghera Superiore and Inferiore, are continued.

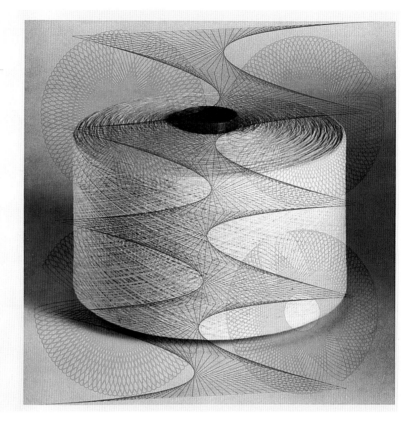

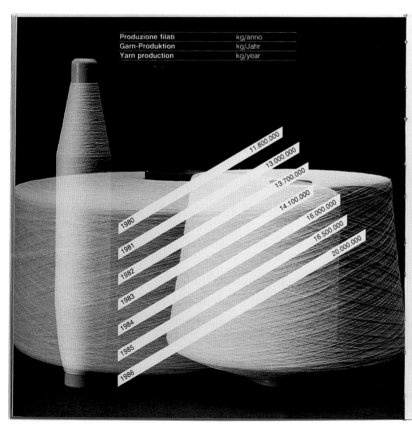

Produzione filati	kg/anno
Garn-Produktion	kg/Jahr
Yarn production	kg/year

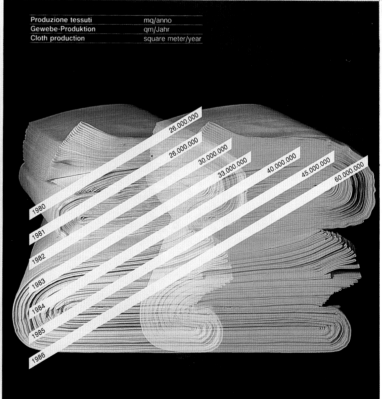

Produzione tessuti	mq/anno
Gewebe-Produktion	qm/Jahr
Cloth production	square meter/year

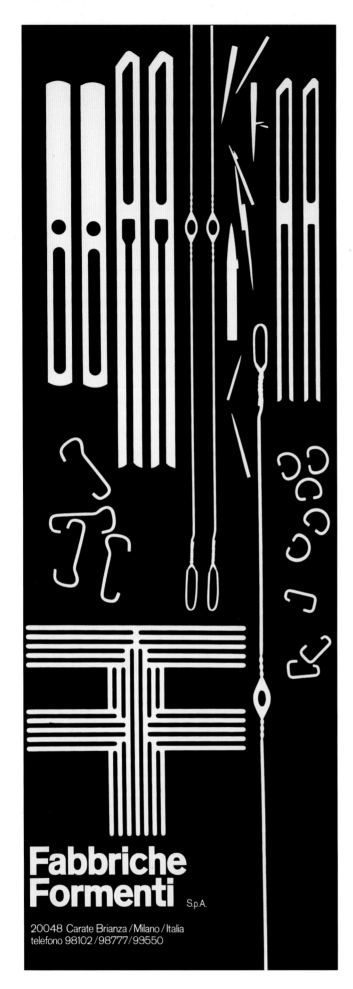

Fabbriche Formenti
advertisement, 1971
315 x 115 mm

Portfolio: Food Industry

As had occurred in the designs for the publishing industry, which developed into sub-classes, designs for the food industry also grouped into specific trends. Female emancipation gave millions of women access to higher levels of education. The resulting introduction into the work world of the working and lower-middle classes altered social roles within the family as well as eating habits. It became increasingly necessary to save time on shopping and the concentration of all commodities (not just indispensable articles but also luxury items) in a single place allowed this. When the first supermarkets opened, the food industry rapidly became an important national production sector and in the space of a few decades small shops were replaced. The opening of the Esselunga supermarkets by the industrialist Caprotti, and Max Huber's design of its logo, were a foretaste of today's reality, where the multiplication of supply in an increasingly global market is leading to the 'hyper'-market and the possibility of shopping citadels.

Another significant factor was the increase in leisure time and the growth in the number of restaurants, American-style bars, etc. Huber designed for a variety of customers in this field. His image for Frisia water, indicating the nature of water through chromatic variations, remains unsurpassed and was only restyled a few years ago; the superimposition of sans serif fonts held true to Huber's style, even in such a mass market. By contrast, the communication for Grassotti, the liqueur manufacturer, and that for Besana, the icecream manufacturer, revealed an unexpected irony. The small icecream cones that turn into visual texture – designed by Huber's wife Aoi Kono – and the large, almost childish pictures of fruit, transform everyday subjects into archetypal images, by opening up to a language similar to that of television cartoons.

top
Grassotti: Whisky
label, c. 1947
115 x 105 mm

centre
Grassotti: Whisky
label, c. 1947
13 x 20 mm

bottom
Grassotti: Extra Old Rhum
label, c. 1947
50 x 170 mm

opposite top
Grassotti: Cherry Brandy, Peach Brandy, Apricot Brandy
labels, c. 1947
60 x 45 mm

opposite centre
Grassotti: Special Cherry Brandy
labels, 1947
65 x 110 mm

opposite bottom
Grassotti: Special Cherry Brandy, Extra Apricot Brandy
labels, 1947
70 x 110 mm

top and bottom left
Grassotti
labels, c. 1947
70 x 70 mm

bottom right
Grassotti
label, c. 1947
155 x 115 mm

opposite
Grassotti
poster, c. 1947
1280 x 905 mm

212   Max Huber

top
Biffi
menu covers, 1960
265 x 115 mm

bottom
**Gonzales American
Snack Bar**
leaflet, 1960
315 x 240 mm

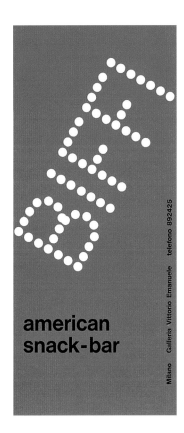

american
snack-bar

Milano   Galleria Vittorio Emanuele   telefono 892425

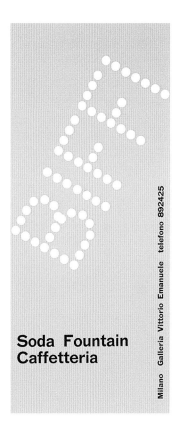

Soda Fountain
Caffetteria

Milano   Galleria Vittorio Emanuele   telefono 892425

MILANO - Via Fabio Filzi 25
Telefono 662888

top
Besana
brochure covers, 1964–6
295 x 210 mm

bottom and opposite right
Besana
brochure inside pages,
1964–6
295 x 420 mm

opposite left
Besana
logo variations, 1960

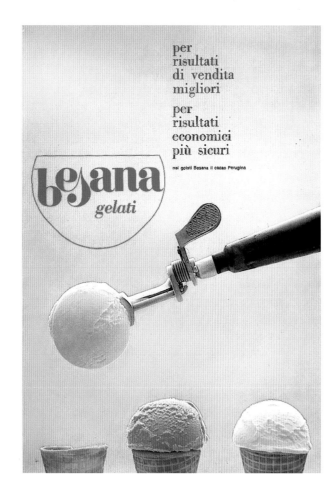

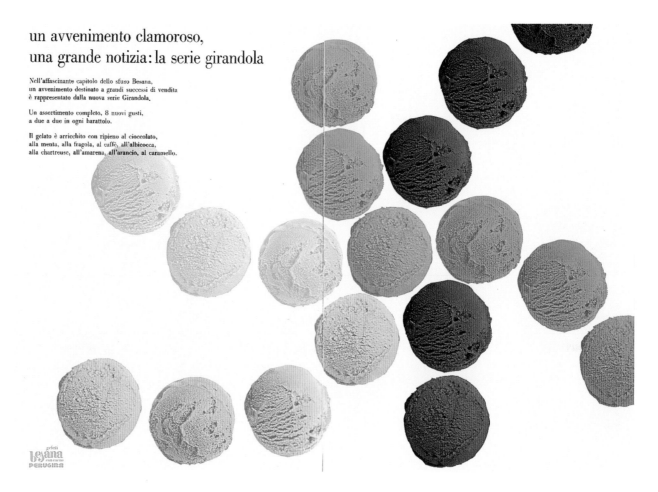

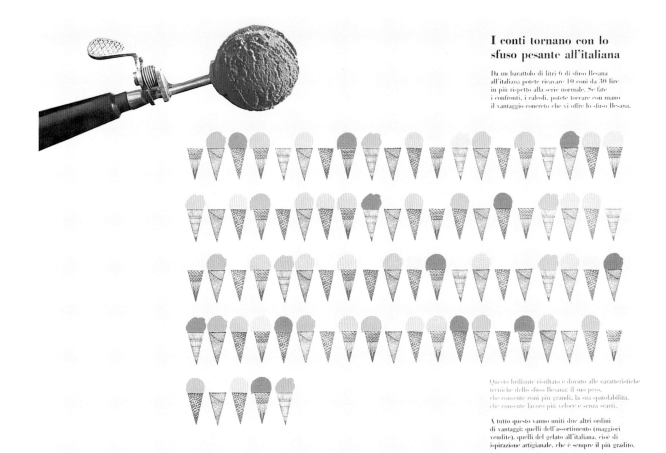

I conti tornano con lo sfuso pesante all'italiana

Da un barattolo di litri 6 di sfuso Besana
all'italiana potete ricavare 10 coni da 30 lire
in più rispetto alla serie normale. Se fate
i confronti, i calcoli, potete toccare con mano
il vantaggio concreto che vi offre lo sfuso Besana.

Questo brillante risultato è dovuto alle caratteristiche
tecniche dello sfuso Besana: il suo peso,
che consente coni più grandi, la sua spatolabilità,
che consente lavoro più veloce e senza scarti.

A tutto questo vanno uniti due altri ordini
di vantaggi: quelli dell'assortimento (maggiori
vendite), quelli del gelato all'italiana, cioè di
ispirazione artigianale, che è sempre il più gradito.

Da aprile ad agosto la Besana organizza vaste campagne
di promozione vendita di gelati eccezionali.
Si tratta di gelati originali, anche di nuove formule,
di idee destinate ad attrarre l'attenzione delle masse, e
a suscitare l'interesse di tutti.
Il punto di vendita Besana ha, anche per questo,
la massima assistenza dell'Azienda,
venendosi a trovare in una posizione di vantaggio
nei confronti dei concorrenti.

con le novità **besana**
sarete fuori concorrenza

i grandi successi e le novità
portate all'attenzione di tutto il pubblico ogni mese
per tutta la stagione.

top
Montalbano
menu covers, 1989
325 x 165 mm

bottom
Prosecco Lucini
study for label, 1987
80 x 120 mm

MENU INVERNO

MENU ESTATE

Portfolio: Stationery

In 1877, a law was passed making elementary education compulsory in Italy and this gave an extraordinary boost to the printing industry, especially in the north; the number of printing works rose from 600 to 1,600 between 1860 and 1903, and those they employed increased from 10,000 to 30,000; in 1902, there were 110 Linotype printing machines, whereas in 1898 there had been just one. These activities were most firmly rooted in the north and printing industries large and small also acted as publishing houses – Salani, Le Monnier, Zanichelli, Loescher, Treves, Sonzogno, Ricordi, etc. Some of the best printing industries appeared in Milan between the wars, partly thanks to the creation of the first printing courses by the Società Tipografica Milanese, absorbed by the Scuola del Libro della Società Umanitaria in 1904. Skilled labour and the publication of the journal *Risorgimento Grafico* in 1902, followed by Attilio Rossi's *Campo Grafico* in 1933, and the presence of a figure such as Raffaello Bertieri, theorist and champion of printing as an artform in itself, placed Milan at the vanguard of an unprecedented rebirth of activities linked to printing.

The interwar period saw the appearance of Alfieri & Lacroix, Nava Arti Grafiche, Arti Grafiche Amilcare Pizzi and Bassoli Arti Grafiche. All these firms turned to the young designers working in the city. Antonio Boggeri was the product quality manager of Alfieri & Lacroix until 1933, when he opened his own studio, and, after the Second World War, both Bassoli and Nava had extraordinary collaborators working on initiatives in a far more advanced role than that of mere execution. Michele Provinciali produced the review *Imago*, in a numbered series, for Bassoli; this was a fine example of the potential of printing at the service of writers and poets of the calibre of Leonardo Sinisgalli. Max Huber helped to define the identity of Nava Arti Grafiche, creating its logo and image, including details such as the positioning of the logo on company vehicles. He was one of the first to produce some memorable calendars – such as *Il Coccodrillo* (Crocodile) in 1960 – published again from 2005. In the 1960s, the Nava Press division was flanked by the new Nava Design, which concentrated on the production of calendars and diaries, as well as quality accessories for the office; it turned to creators such as Silvio Coppola, Giulio Confalonieri and Pino Tovaglia as well as Max Huber, and secured itself a qualified niche market while also venturing into the international sphere in New York and São Paulo.

top
Nava
study for logo, 1961
345 x 335 mm

opposite top
Christmas Card for Nava
1963
105 x 215 mm

opposite centre left
**Nava: Calendari
(Calendars)**
product branding, c. 1970,

opposite bottom left
Nava
advertisement, c. 1970,
300 x 210 mm

opposite right
Nava
advertisement, 1961,
315 x 235 mm

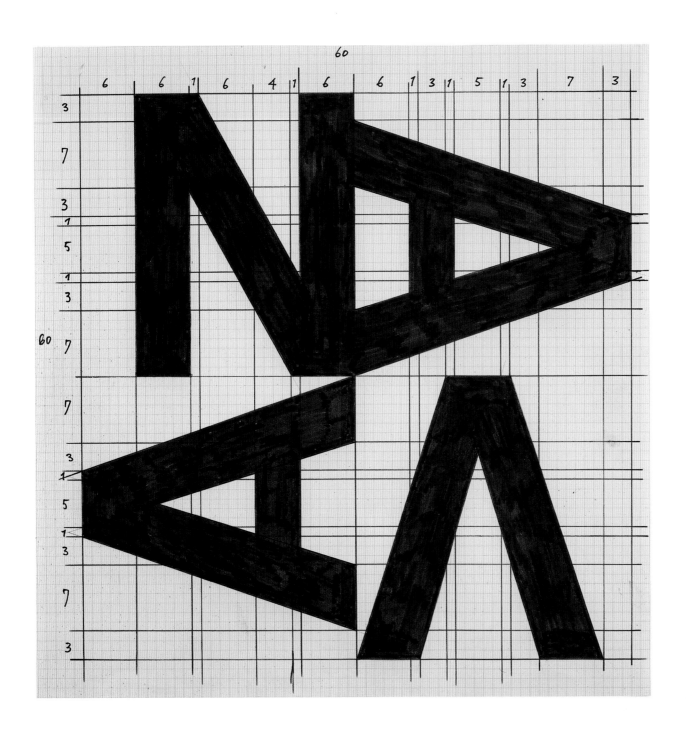

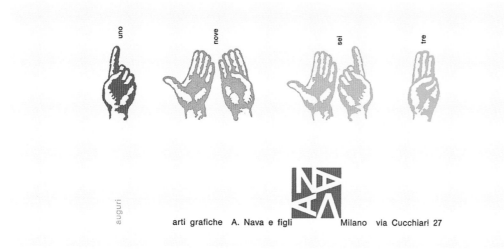

auguri

arti grafiche A. Nava e figli   Milano via Cucchiari 27

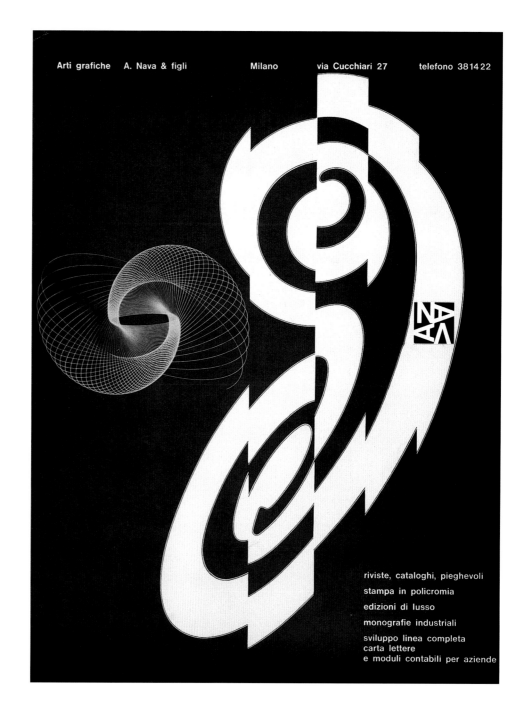

Nava
poster, 1967
500 x 700 mm

opposite
Nava
advertisement, 1969
300 x 210 mm

QUESTO è un es
empio. il campio
nario CARATTERI vuol
dirvi anche TANTI AUGU
RI per l'anno 1967 dalle grafiche
Nava Milano tipografia / litografia
! ,.;. ? & ' via Rucellai 30/D
telefoni 2578208/10/12

grafiche A. Nava

20126 Milano
Via Rucellai 30/D
telefoni 2578208/210/212

max huber
milano 2
via gerolamo morone 6
telefono 793380

opposite
Nava
calendars, 1950s–60s

top
Nava
diary, 1970s
240 x 170 mm

bottom
Nava
diary, 1987
160 x 85 mm

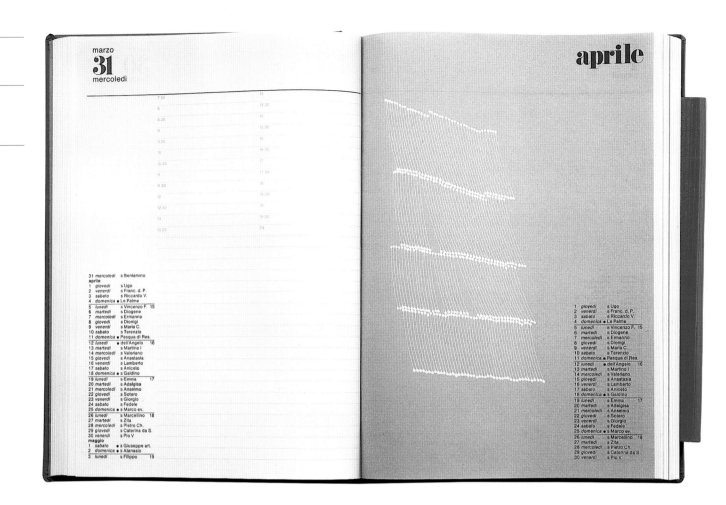

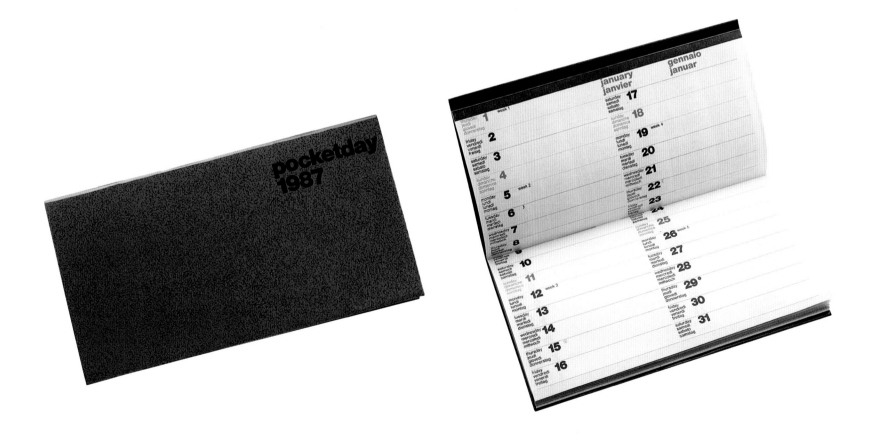

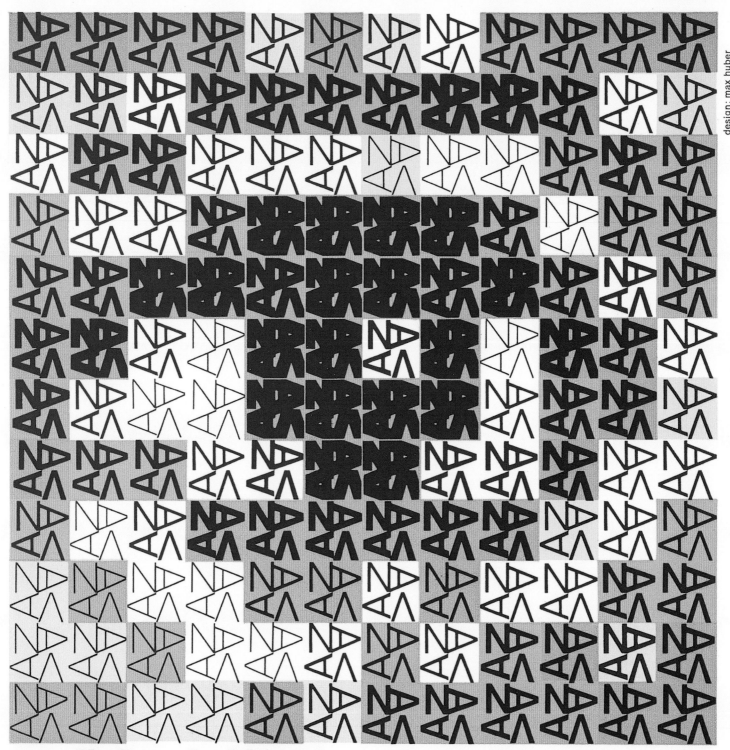

grafiche A. Nava
tipografia/litografia___20126 Milano___via Rucellai 30/D___telefono 2570251

opposite
Nava
advertisement, 1970
200 x 180 mm

top and bottom
Nava
posters, 1973
240 x 170 mm

anche Martin Lutero alle   **grafiche A. Nava**
20126 Milano
via Martino Lutero 5 - telefono 2570251

Notes

Essay 1

I am grateful to Mrs Aoi Huber, Max Huber's widow, for welcoming me on a number of occasions into the artist's archive in Chiasso, to Dr Letizia Tedeschi, Accademia di architettura, Mendrisio, for assistance with the bibliography, and to Alan Colquhoun, London, for his help in establishing the final version of this essay.

1 See Gillo Dorfles, *Simbolo, comunicazione, consumo* (Turin, Einaudi, 1962).

2 Roberto Furian et al., 'Max Huber: Viaggio nella memoria perduta', *Grafica & Design*, 19 (1996), pp. 32–41.

3 'Although it is possible to like our creations without fully understanding them, one is scarcely able to extract from them all the pleasure thay can give without at least a little insight into the methods by which they have been evolved … a certain number of relationships which show themselves both in the theme and in the fifteen variations'. See Max Bill, *Quinze Variations sur un même thème*, (Paris, Editions des Chroniques du Jour, 1938) reprinted in Eduard Hüttinger, *Max Bill* (Zurich, abc, 1977).

4 See Filippo Marinetti, 'The Foundation and Manifesto of Futurism', tr. Joshua C. Taylor in Herschel B. Chipp, *Theories of Modern Art: A Source Book by Artists and Critics* (Berkeley, University of California Press, 1968), pp. 284–89, esp. p. 286; 'Manifeste du futurisme', *Le Figaro*, 20 February 1909. On the 'teatri di massa', see, for example, Jeffrey T. Schnapp, *18 BL: Mussolini e l'opera d'arte di massa* (Cernusco s./M, Garzanti, 1996), an expanded Italian translation of *Staging Fascism: 18 BL and the Theater of Masses for Masses* (Stanford University Press, 1996).

5 On this, see, for example, Luciano Caramel, 'Gli astratti: Tra idea e prassi' in Marco Abate and Domenico Pertocoli, *Anni trenta. Arte e Cultura in Italia* (Milan, Mazzotta, 1982), pp. 151–74.

6 Vance Packard, *The Hidden Persuaders* (New York, D. McKay, 1957).

7 Max Huber, untitled lecture manuscript, 1987: 'Scrive McLuhan, un bambino che sta ancora nel seggiolino oggi riceve molte più informazioni dal mondo attraverso la televisione che i nonni in tutta la loro vita.' Thanks to the worldwide success of McLuhan's books such as *The Gutenberg Galaxy: The Making of Typographic Man* (University of Toronto Press, 1962), *Understanding Media: The Extensions of Man* (New York, McGraw-Hill, 1964) and *The Medium Is the Massage: An Inventory of Effects* (New York, Random House, 1967), such concepts were general knowledge at the time.

8 Max Huber, untitled lecture manuscript: 'operatore artigiano, quasi preistorico della comunicazione visiva'.

9 Marshall McLuhan, *The Mechanical Bride: Folklore of Industrial Man* (Boston, Beacon Press, 1967), p. 98.

10 See Daniel Robbins (ed.), *The Independent Group: Postwar Britain and the Aesthetics of Plenty* (Cambridge, Mass and London, MIT Press, 1990). Astonishingly, McLuhan's book was not published in England until 1967; despite surprisingly similar interests, it seems not to have featured in the discussions of early British Pop artists.

11 See Arthur A. Cohen, *Herbert Bayer: The Complete Work* (Cambridge, Mass and London, MIT Press, 1984).

12 See Max Huber, 'L'avvenire della grafica: collaborare con i pubblicisti' (interview with Tom Granich), *Fatti*, January–March 1962, pp.25–32. In fact, scepticism with respect to market research as promoted by American advertisers such as Walter J Thompson had been a constant theme in the orbit of the 'New Graphic Art' in Switzerland. An early example is the art historian Peter Meyer's observation of 1932 'that the psycho-technic evaluation of advertising projects merely takes account of and thereby sanctions the existing bad taste' ('dass die psychotechnische Begutachtung von Reklameentwürfen lediglich den bestehenden schlechten Geschmack als massgebend feststellt und damit sanktioniert'), in 'Reklamegraphik und Psychotechnik', *Das Werk*, 12 (1932), pp. 383f. An extremely well documented discussion of this dilemma between 'good design' and 'good selling' as discussed in Switzerland can be found in Christoph Bignens, *American Way of Life. Architektur, Comics, Design, Werbung* (Sulgen, Niggli, 2003), pp. 153–79.

13 Alexander Dorner, *The Way Beyond 'Art': The Work of Herbert Bayer* (New York, Wittenborn, 1947). In the German edition, which appeared somewhat later, the chapter on Bayer was dropped. On Dorner's place in the history of design theory, see Manfredo Tafuri, *Teorie e storie dell'architettura* (Bari, Laterza, 1970), pp. 63–67; on Dorner and Bayer, see Stanislaus von Moos, 'Modern Art Gets Down to Business' in *Herbert Bayer: Das künstlerische Werk, 1918–1938* (Berlin, Mann, 1982), pp. 93–104. The best analysis of the case is by Joan Ockman, 'The Road Not Taken: Alexander Dorner's Way Beyond Art' in Robert Somol (ed.), *Autonomy and Ideology: Positioning an Avant-Garde in America* (New York, Monacelli, 1997), pp. 80–120.

14 Dorner, *The Way Beyond 'Art'*, p. 181.

15 On the influence of Surrealism – and especially of Max Ernst – on American advertising, see Werner Spies, 'Der Surrealismus in den USA. Dokumente einer Faszination', in *Max Ernst. Retrospektive* (Munich, Prestel, 1979), pp. 97–120; on Dalí, see *Dalí and Mass Culture* (Barcelona and Figueres, Fundació la Caixa and Fundació Gala-Salvador Dalí, 2004). One of the ideologues of 'New Graphics' who explicitly rejected the Surrealist fashion was Richard Paul Lohse in 'Surrealismus und Gebrauchsgrafik', *Chamäleon*, nos. 9–10 (1947), pp. 60f.

16 Dorner, *The Way Beyond 'Art'*, p. 181.

17 James Joyce, *Ulysses* (Paris, Shakespeare and Company, 1928), pp. 130, 640, 676.

18 On the role of 'ornament' as a base of modern art see Markus Brüderlin (ed.), *Ornament und Abstraktion* (Riehen, Fondation Beyeler, 2001) as well as Jürg Gleiter, 'Kritische Theorie des Ornaments. Zum Statuswandel der Aesthetik in der architektonischen Moderne' (Bauhaus Universität-Weimar, 2002). I discussed some of the problems involved in 'Ornament und Common Sense. Ueber Max Bill und Peter Meyer' in Katharina Corsepius, Daniela Mondini, Darko Senekovic, Lino Sibillano and Samuel Vitali, *Opus Tesselatum. Modi und Grenzgänge der Kunstwissenschaft. Festschrift für Peter Cornelius Claussen* (Hildesheim/Zurich/New York, Georg Olms, 2004), pp. 465–82.

19 See Giovanni Anceschi, 'Le tre attualità di Max Huber', *Linea Grafica* (1994), pp. 10–21: 'Huber va considerato la figura di progettista più rilevante della produzione grafica italiana'.

20 Cornelius van Eesteren, 'Karl Moser + 28 Februari 1936', *De 8 en opbouw*, 7–8 (1936).

21 In the 1950s, Oliviero Toscani, among many others, would also study at the school before stirring up the Italian art and design world with his work at Benetton decades later. Oliviero Toscani, *La pub est une charogne qui nous sourit* (Paris, Éditions Hoëbeke, 1995).

22 Alfred Roth (ed.), *La nouvelle architecture/Die neue Architektur/The New Architecture* (Zurich, H. Girsberger, 1940).

23 The most complete survey of the phenomenon of the 'Swiss style' in commercial design, including a detailed chronology and extensive bibliography, is Christoph Bignens, *Swiss Style: Die grosse Zeit der Gebrauchsgrafik in der Schweiz, 1914–1964*, (Zurich, Chronos, 2000).

24 See Antonio Boggeri, 'Advertising Art in Post-War Italy', *Graphis*, 18 (1947), pp. 148–53; Rudolf Hostettler, 'Kleiner Mailänder Druckspiegel', *Schweizer Graphische Mitteilungen*, 2 (November 1948), pp. 457–60.

25 See pp. 80–102, 'The Milan Years' by Mara Campana in the present volume.

26 For an earlier attempt in this direction see Stanislaus von Moos and Eduard F. Sekler (eds.), *The Other Twenties. Themes in Art and Advertising 1920–1930* (Cambridge, Mass, Carpenter Center for the Visual Arts, Harvard University, 1975). On Aby Warburg and his fundamental role in the history of cultural studies and especially on his concept of the *Bilderatlas*, see Werner Hofmann, Georg Syamken and Martin Warnke, *Die Menschenrechte des Auges. Ueber Aby Warburg*, (Frankfurt, Europäische Verlagsanstalt, 1980) as well as more recently, Kurt W Forster, 'Warburgs Versunkenheit' in Robert Galitz and Brita Reimers (eds.), *Aby M. Warburg. 'Ekstatische Nymphe… trauernder Flussgott'. Portrait eines Gelehrten*, (Hamburg, Dölling und Galitz Verlag, 1995), pp. 184–206. The reference biography on Warburg is still Ernst H Gombrich, *Aby Warburg. Eine intellektuelle Biographie*, (Frankfurt, Europäische Verlagsanstalt, 1970).

27 Sport – men and women on the sports field – had of course been a central theme in early Soviet propaganda art. See, for example, Christiane Bauermeister-Paetzel and Sylvia Wetzel, 'Ein Huhn ist kein Vogel, ein Weib ist kein Mensch. Die neue Frau in der sowjetischen Kunst zur Zeit der Industrialisierung und Kollektivierung' in Christian Borngräber et al. (eds.), *'Kunst in die Produktion!' Materialien* (Berlin, Neue Gesellschaft für Bildende Kunst, 1977), pp. 24–49.

28 Adolf Max Vogt, *Russische und Französische Revolutionsarchitektur, 1917–1789: Zur Einwirkung des Marxismus und des Newtonismus auf die Bauweise* (Cologne, DuMont, 1974), pp. 141–94, esp. pp. 163ff.

29 By contrast, compare the GM advertisements that circulated in Switzerland in the 1950s, featuring flashy American cars, which were of course mocked by the 'enlightened'; see Christoph Bignens, *American Way of Life: Architektur, Comics, Design, Werbung*, p. 178.

30 On this, see Christian Borngräber, 'Hans Schmidt und Hannes Meyer in Moskau', *werk.archithese*, 23–24 (1978), pp. 37–40.

31 Designed in 1928–31 by Max Ernst Haefeli, Rudolf Steiger, Emil Roth, Paul Artaria and Hans Schmidt.

32 On Neubühl see Ueli Marbach and Arthur Rüegg, *Werkbund-Siedlung Neubühl* (Zurich, gta, 1990) and on the Doldertal flats, see Rüegg, Siegfried Giedion and Alfred Roth, *Die Doldertalhäuser* (Zurich, gta, 1996). On the socio-political context see Stanislaus von Moos, 'Die Moderne im Sandkasten: Anmerkungen zur Schweizer Architektur der Jahre 1929-1941' in Claude Lichtenstein et al. (eds.), *O. R. Salvisberg: Die andere Moderne* (Zurich, gta, 1985), pp. 140–47.

33 Stanislaus von Moos, 'Eine Avantgarde geht in die Produktion: Die Zürcher CIAM-Gruppe und der "Wohnbedarf"' in Helmuth Gsöllpointner, Angela Hareiter, and Laurids Ortner (eds.), *Design ist unsichtbar* (Vienna, Löcker, 1981), pp. 195–208.

34 This work would later appear on a cover of the journal *Domus* (June 1946), which Huber designed.

35 Roland Barthes, 'The Plates of The Encyclopedia' in *New Critical Essays*, tr. Richard Howard (New York, Hill & Wang, 1980), p. 28.

36 As the symbol for the Compasso d'oro, the European design award institutionalized by La Rinascente in 1954, the compass would enjoy an important renaissance (see pp. 90–91 and 115 in the present volume).

37 For more recent discussions of the Schweizerische Landesausstellung, and a bibliography of recent literature, see Karin Gimmi, 'Von der Kunst, mit Architektur Staat zu machen: Armin Meili und die LA '39' in Georg Kohler and Stanislaus von Moos (eds.), *Expo-Syndrom? Materialien zur Landesausstellung, 1883–2002* (Zurich, vdf, 2002), pp. 157–78.

38 A more discriminating 'first-hand' presentation is found in Peter Meyer, 'Die Architektur der Landesausstellung: Kritische Besprechung', *Das Werk*, 11 (1939), pp. 321–52.

39 Konrad Farner, *Hans Erni: Ein Maler unserer Zeit* (Zurich, Vereinigung 'Kultur und Volk', 1945), pp. 66f. For a more recent interpretation of the mural, see Stanislaus von Moos, 'Hans Erni and the Streamline Decade', *The Journal of Decorative and Propaganda Arts*, 19 (1993), pp. 120–49, and idem, 'Peintre officiel maudit: Hans Erni, Konrad Farner und der kritische Landigeist' in idem, *Nicht Disneyland, und andere Aufsätze über Modernität und Nostalgie* (Zurich, Scheidegger & Spiess, 2004), pp. 77–94.

40 Cf. 'Biografia' in *Max Huber: Pittore/Maler/Painter* (Mendrisio, Vignalunga, 1991), n.p., which mentions his collaboration in 1942 with Erni on poster designs and a banknote programme for the Swiss national bank but not his work on the 'Landi' painting.

41 The most precise assessment of Huber's work as a painter – namely, Luciano Caramel, 'Max Huber: Il laboratorio della pittura' in *Max Huber: Pittore/Maler/Painter*, n.p. – in my view places too much emphasis on the non-objective components of his oeuvre. Likewise, Christoph Bignens divides 'Swiss style' into a 'functional' tendency ('constructive graphic art'), centred in Zurich on the one hand, and a freer, 'sometimes amusing … illustrative graphic art', centred in Basel on the other. The case of Erni, who was active in Lucerne, is thus largely left out; see Bignens, *Swiss Style*. Several useful biographical details are related in Dieter Bachmann, 'Spuren: Ermittlungen über Werner Bischof nebst einer Einführung des Ermittlers', *Du*, 9 (September 1990), pp. 18–23.

42 On 'Kontinuität' see Werner Spies, *Kontinuität: Granit-Monolith von Max Bill* (Frankfurt am Main, Busche Verlagsgesellschaft, 1986). The bibliography on Max Bill is extensive. The best survey is Eduard Hüttinger, *Max Bill* (Zurich, abc, 1977); but for an interesting critical discussion see also Carlo Quintavalle, *Max Bill* (Università Comune Provincia di Parma, 1977).

43 Ettore Sottsass, Jr., 'per qualcuno può essere lo spazio' in *Arte astratta e arte concreta* (Milan, Alfieri e Lacroix, 1947), pp. 22–25, esp. p. 25: 'uno puo dire tranquillamente che i popoli della Grecia non esistono senza il mare e il mare è la loro grande storia. La nostra grande storia io penso che sia la velocità.'

44 See Anceschi, 'L'ideogramma cinestetico di Max Huber', *Linea Grafica*, 290 (March 1994).

45 On this, see the important essay by Bruno Reichlin, 'Konkrete Kunst an der Arbeit'/'L'art concret au travail', *Faces*, 15 (1990), pp. 4–6, 18–24.

46 See Jan Morgenthaler, *Der Mann mit der Hand im Auge: Die Lebensgeschichte von Karl Geiser; Bildhauer, Zeichner und Photograph* (Zurich, Limmat-Verlag, 1988). The monument was not executed until 1964.

47 Reichlin, 'Konkrete Kunst an der Arbeit'.

48 Quoted in Reichlin, op. cit.

49 Vladimir Mayakovsky, *Dlia golosa* [For the voice]; *konstruktor knigi El Lisitskii* [constructed by El Lissitzky] (Berlin, Tip. Lutze & Vogt, 1923).

50 Max Bill, 'Von der abstrakten zur konkreten Kunst', quoted from the Italian translation, 'dall'arte astratta all'arte concreta' in *Arte astratta e concreta*: 'contenuto e forma del quadro formano un'unità autonoma. Non si può più paragonare questo quadro ai dipinti tradizionali. La sua struttura, i sui elementi, non sono astratti dall'ambiente in cui viviamo. Null'altro ha valore oltre ciò che si può vedere, fin tanto che non vengano prodotte e suscitate tensione e atmosfera con colori e forme, fin tanto che il complesso del quadro non si componga in se stessa in unità artistica.'

51 *Arte astratta e arte concreta*, p. 13.

52 Max Bill, 'konkrete gestaltung' in *Zeitprobleme in der Schweizer Malerei und Plastik* (Zurich, Kunsthaus, 1936).

53 See Béla Stetzer, 'Modulare Ordnung: Eine Vision des industriellen Zeitalters' in Richard Paul Lohse (ed.), *Konstruktive Gebrauchsgrafik* (Ostfildern-Ruit, Richard Paul Lohse-Stiftung, Hatje Cantz Verlag, 1999), pp. 153–81.

54 In 1941, Huber contributed a work to a portfolio of ten sheets issued by Allianz, '5 construktionen + 5 composi-tionen'; see 'Biografia' in *Max Huber: Pittore/Maler/Painter*.

55 From the catalogue's foreword it appears that the exhibitors made a virtue out of necessity; being unable to show any works by Concrete artists of the first generation such as Moholy-Nagy, Mondrian, Doesburg and others, they perhaps had no choice but to focus on the Swiss contribution, which was relatively easy to document. Switzerland was the 'country that has made the greatest contribution to Concrete art', as they put it ('la nazione che ha dato il maggior contributo all'arte concreta') and Bill 'the most productive Swiss Concrete artist' ('il più produttivo artista concreto svizzero'), p. 3.

56 In this context, see Hans Heinz Holz, 'Max Huber: "konkret" weiterdenken' in *Max Huber* (Zurich, Helmhaus Zürich, 1990), pp. 9–13.

57 As Max Bill described a work by Leo Leuppi in 'Dall'arte astratta all'arte concreta' .

58 For a particularly insightful discussion of these visual techniques see Andreas Haus, *Moholy-Nagy. Fotos und Fotogramme* (Munich, Schirmer-Mosel, 1978), pp. 23ff.

59 Anceschi, 'L'ideogramma cinestetico di Max Huber'.

60 Karl Gerstner and Markus Kutter, *Die neue Graphik* (Teufen, Niggli, 1959), p. 118–9. Needless to say, the remark also sheds light on the programme of the advertising agency Gerstner+Kutter (later: GGK), founded in Basel that same year.

Essay 2

1 See *Lo Studio Boggeri* (Milan, Electa, 1981).

2 See Filippo Tommaso Marinetti and Tato, 'Manifesto della fotografia Futurista', 11 April 1930.

3 See Carlo Bertelli, 'La fedeltà incostante' in Bertelli and Giulio Bollati, *Storia d'Italia. L'immagine fotografica 1845–1945*. (Torino, Einaudi, 1979).

4 Luigi Veronesi, *Ferrania* (Milan, 1956).

5 See Bertelli, 'La fedeltà incostante'.

6 Gio Ponti, *Domus*, 53 (1932).

7 Roberto Leydi, *Max Huber: Grafica 1940/1990* (Chiasso, Sala Diego Chiesa, 1990).

8 See Roberto Leydi, 'L'uomo che cambiò i giornali' in *L'Europeo*, XXX:36 (5 September 1974).

Essay 3

1 See various authors, *Das Goldene Buch der LA 1939*, (Zurich, Verkehrsverlag, 1939).

2 Various authors, 'Max Huber (1919-1992) Costruire giocando con i segni. La grafica negli allestimenti', from a conversation between Giampiero Bosoni, Sonia Calzoni and Max Huber in the latter's home-studio in Sagno, Ticino (Switzerland) on 4 May 1990, *Progex – design e architetture espositive*, 10 (May 1994).

3 Ibid.

4 Ivo Allas and Bosoni, 'Il progetto Svizzera nelle esposizioni internazionali (1924–1939)', *Rassegna* 62 (1995).

5 From the detailed biography, edited by Huber himself, published in *Max Huber: Pittore/Maler/Painter* (Mendrisio, Vignalunga, 1991).

6 Various authors, 'Max Huber (1919–1992)'.

7 Various authors, *Catalogo della VII Triennale* (Milan, 1940), p. 153.

8 Documents in the Archivio Boggeri conserved by Anna Boggeri in Melide, Ticino (Switzerland).

9 Various authors, *Visual design. Cinquant'anni di produzione in Italia* (Milan, Idealibri, 1984), picture no. 61.

10 See *Max Huber: Progetti grafici 1936–1981* (Milan, Electa, 1982).

11 See Biography from *Max Huber: Pittore/Maler/Painter*.

12 See Bosoni, 'La ricostruzione edilizia e l'arredo popolare' in Vittorio Gregotti with Bosoni, Manolo De Giorgi and Andrea Nulli (eds.), *Il disegno del prodotto industriale Italia 1860–1980* (Electa, Milan, 1981).

13 See various authors, 'Max Huber (1919–1992)'.

14 Various authors, *Ottava Triennale di Milano. Catalogo-guida* (Milan, 1947).

15 See Sergio Polano, *Mostrare, l'allestimento in Italia dagli anni Venti agli anni Ottanta* (Milan, Edizioni Lybra Immagine, 1988), p. 76.

16 Gillo Dorfles, 'arte astratta e concreta', *Domus*, 217 (January 1947).

17 Sergio Polano, *Achille Castiglioni tutte le opere 1938–2000* (Milan, Electa, 2001).

18 Sonia Calzoni, 'BBPR con Max Huber e Franco Buzzi Ceriani: La forma dell'utile alla IX Esposizione Triennale di Milano, 1951', *Progex – design & architetture espositive*, 4 (September 1990).

19 Ibid.

20 See *Rassegna Pubblicitaria* (May 1959): 'Sia nella progettazione dell'ambiente che nella realizzazione grafica manca volutamente ogni ricerca di composizione e di gusto, di materiali e di colore, che si ritrova sempre negli allestimenti più moderni e raffinati. La grande parete è solo caratterizzata dal gioco della luce colorata e dal movimento, che richiama il visitatore in un ambiente pieno di vita, senza convenzioni, quasi divertente e che ricorda i saloni affollati di giovani attorno ai flippers, ai Juke-box'.

21 Polano, *Achille Castiglioni*, p. 190.

22 Ibid., p. 197.

23 Ibid., p. 228.

24 Lisa Licitra Ponti, 'In attesa del Duemila', *Domus*, 461 (April 1968), pp. 26–29.

25 Achille Castiglioni, 'Max Huber', in *Watches*, (Officina Alessi, 1989).

Index

Page numbers in *italics* refer to picture captions

Acknowledgements

The Publisher wishes to thank Mrs Aoi Kono
for her invaluable suggestions, Giampiero
Bosoni, Mara Campana and Stanislaus von
Moos for their various contributions beyond
the authorship of their own essays, the max,
binia + jakob bill foundation for their help
and generosity, and everyone at the Max
Huber.Kono Foundation for their assistance.

Mrs Aoi Kono would like to especially thank
Alan Fletcher, Stanislaus von Moos, the
Studio Achille Castiglioni and René Burri for
their contributions and invaluable advice.
She would also like to thank Hans Dieter
Reichert, Giampiero Bosoni, Mara Campana
and Gianluca Poletti for their assistance
with this book.

The Max Huber.Kono Foundation would like
to acknowledge the generous contribution
of the Alessi Archive, Studio Achille
Castiglioni, Harald Mol, Ugo Mulas, Alfred
Pratelli, Publifoto, the RAI Archive, La
Rinascente Archive, the Milan Triennale
Archive, Toshio Yoshida and Alo Zanetta.

The work of Max Huber featured in this
book can be seen at the:

m.a.x.Museo
Via Dante Alighieri 6
CH 6830 Chiasso
Switzerland

www.maxmuseo.ch